Prima's

GameShark™
Pocket Power Guide
Code Revolution
CodeBoy

® is a registered trademark of Prima Publishing, a
division of Prima Communications, Inc.

PRIMA

Project Editor: **Sara E. Wilson**
Created by: **Prima Creative Services, England**

GameShark is © 1997 InterAct Accessories, Inc. InterAct, GameShark and "Abuse
the Power" are trademarks of STD Manufacturing.

All products and characters mentioned in this book are trademarks of their
respective companies.

Important:
Prima Publishing has made every effort to determine that the information contained
in this book is accurate. However, the publisher makes no warranty, either
expressed or implied, as to the accuracy, effectiveness, or completeness of the
material in this book; nor does the publisher assume liability for damages, either
incidental or consequential, that may result from using the information in this book.
The publisher cannot provide information regarding game play, hints and strategies,
or problems with hardware or software. Questions should be directed to the
support numbers provided by the game and device manufacturers in their
documentation. Some game tricks require precise timing and may require repeated
attempts before the desired result is achieved.

ISBN: 7615-1550-X
Library of Congress Catalog Card Number: 97-69763
Printed in the United States of America

98 99 00 01 HH 10 9 8 7 6 5 4 3 2
Prima Publishing
Rocklin, California
(916) 632-4400
www.primagames.com

Overpower the Hottest Games and Revive the Old Ones.

GameShark is the ultimate game enhancer. With GameShark, you can take your gaming to new levels of fun and excitement. Gain access to hidden characters, weapons and vehicles. Even the odds with infinite health and endless ammo. Obtain those hard-to-find keys with ease. "Put in the fix" so your team always wins. GameShark takes you where you want to go!

How To Use This Book

There are many games that require more than one code to be entered in order to get the desired effect. In these cases, we have labelled each code with the same name so you know to enter the following codes consecutively. All the lines of code must be entered into the Enhancement Entry box for the code to work.

What's Inside

Nintendo 64

AEROFIGHTERS ASSAULT
Infinite Chaffs **8027E017000A**
Infinite Special Weapons **8027E4D20002**

AUTOMOBILI LAMBORGHINI
Infinite Time **800CE76F0063**
100 Points. **800CE7430064**
Extra Vehicles **800985C30001**
Extra Vehicles **800985C50001**
Extra Vehicles **800985C70001**
Extra Vehicles **800985CB0001**
Extra Vehicles **800985CD0001**
Extra Vehicles **800985CF0001**

BOMBERMAN 64
Infinite Lives **802AC6270063**
Stop Timer **802AC6430000**
Infinite Credits **802AC62B0063**
Gems **802AC62F0063**
Battle Mode "In The Gutter" Stage **802AC61F0006**
Battle Mode "In The Gutter" Stage **802AC7030006**
Battle Mode "Sea Sick" Stage **802AC61F0007**
Battle Mode "Sea Sick" Stage **802AC7030007**
Battle Mode "Blizzard Battle" Stage **802AC61F0008**
Battle Mode "Blizzard Battle" Stage **802AC7030008**
Battle Mode "Lost At Sea" Stage **802AC61F0009**
Battle Mode "Lost At Sea" Stage **802AC7030009**

CHAMELEON TWIST
Extra Crowns **802517670015**
Access All Levels **8020850E00FF**
Access All Levels **8020851000FF**

CLAY FIGHTER 63 1/3
Extra Characters/Secret Options **801A2B41000F**

CRUSIN' USA
Always Place 1st 8015022B0001
Unlimited Time 8015094D0045

CRUSIN' USA VERSION 1.1
Always Place 1st 8015034B0001

DARK RIFT
Enable Demitron 80049DF40001
Enable Sonork 80049DF00001

DOOM 64
Always Have BFG 9000 ....800632DB0001
Always Have Chain Gun 800632CF0001
Always Have Chainsaw 800632BB0001
Always Have Double Shotgun 800632CB0001
Always Have Gun 800632C30001
Always Have Missile Launcher 800632D30001
Always Have Plasma Rifle 800632D70001
Always Have Shotgun 800632C70001
Blue Key 8006328F0001
Blue Skull Key 8006329B0001
Gun/Chain Gun Ammo 800632E300FF
Invincible 8006330B0002
Missile Ammo 800632EF0064
Plasma/BFG/Weapons Ammo 800632EB0064
Red Key 800632970001
Red Skull Key 800632A30001
Shotgun Ammo 800632E70064
Yellow Key 800632930001
Yellow Skull Key 8006329F0001
Yellow Key 800632930001
Yellow Skull Key 8006329F0001

DUKE NUKEM 64

Cheat Menu	801012D80001
Cheat Menu	801012DC0001
Cheat Menu	801012E00001
Cheat Menu	801012E40001
Cheat Menu	801012E80001
Expander/Missile Launcher	812A5AC00101
Have All Keys	802A5A47000F
Infinite Expander Ammo	802A5A0D00FF
Infinite Grenades	802A5A0700FF
Infinite Jet Pack	812A5A8E0640
Infinite Laser Trip Bomb Ammo	802A5A1300FF
Infinite Missiles	802A5A0F00FF
Infinite Pipe Bomb Ammo	802A5A0900FF
Infinite Plasma Ammo	802A5A1100FF
Infinite Shrinker Ammo	802A5A0B00FF
Infinite SMG Ammo	802A5A0500FF
Pipe Bombs/Shrinker	812A5ABE0101
Plasma Cannon/Laser Trip Bombs	812A5AC20101
SMGs/Grenade Launcher	812A5ABC0101

EXTREME G

100 Points	80167C370063
Anti-Gravity + Fish Eye Lens	80095F6F000A
Anti-Gravity Mode	80095F6F0008
Boulder Mode	80095F6F0001
Boulder Mode + Fish Eye Lens	80095F6F0003
Boulder Mode + Wireframe Mode	80095F6F0011
Extreme Mode	80095F6E0002
Fish Eye Lens	80095F6F0002

FIFA SOCCER 64
Home Team Scores 0 .801190470000
Away Team Scores 0 .801190430000
Home Team Scores 9 .801190470009
Away Team Scores 9 .801190430009

GOLDENEYE
2XGrenade Launchers 8006966E0001
2XHunting Knife 800696710001
2XLaser 800696720001
2XRC-P90 . . . . .8006966F0001
2XRocket Launchers 8006966D0001
2XThrowing Knife 800696700001
All Guns 800696530001
Bond Invisible 8006965A0001
DK Mode 8006965C0001
Enemy Rockets 8006966C0001
Fast Animation 8006966A0001
Gold PP7 800696650001
Golden Gun 800696630001
Infinite Ammo 8006965B0001
Invincible 800696520001
Laser 800696620001
Line Mode 800696570001
Magnum 800696610001
No Radar (Multi) 800696670001
Paint Ball Mode 8006965F0001
Silver PP7 800696640001
Slow Animation 8006966B0001
Tiny Bond 8006965E0001
Turbo Mode 800696680001

HEXEN
Axe/Staff/Frost Shards 8013DB7700FF
Hammer/Firestorm/Arc of Death 8013DB7900FF
Infinite Blue Mana 8013DB7D00CF
Infinite Green Mana .8013DB7F00CF
Invincibility 8113DB4CFFFF
Quietus/Wraithverge/Blood... . . . . .8013DB7B00FF

MACE—THE DARK AGES
Extra Characters 8007F9F80001
Infinite Health P1 . . . . .8008B1E70064
Infinite Health P2 . . . . .8008AE5F0064
No Health P1 . . . . .8008B1E70000
No Health P2 . . . . .8008AE5F0000
Z Trigger Deathblow P1 . . . . .D007CD2A0020
Z Trigger Deathblow P1 . . . . .8008AE5F0000
R Button Health Restore P1 . . . . .D007CD2B0010
R Button Health Restore P1 . . . . .8008B1E70064

MARIO KART 64
No Laps to Race 811643900000
No Laps to Race 811643920002

MORTAL KOMBAT TRILOGY
Player 1 No Energy .8016984D0000
Player 1 Unlimited Energy 8016984D00A6
Player 2 No Energy .80169B210000
Player 2 Unlimited Energy 80169B2100A6

MULTI RACING CHAMPIONSHIP
Infinite Time D0094E97000A
Infinite Time 80094E970064
Low Course Time 8009483B0000
Always Place 1st 800A960F0000

PILOT WINGS
Infinite Fuel Gyrocopter 803628210081
Low Timer 803627500001

SAN FRANCISCO RUSH
GS Button for Extra Track 881000500006
Auto Abort Disable .800F40780001
Change Textures 800F3DA00001
Cones to Mines 800F3F880001
No Collisions 800F40500001
Resurrect In Place 800F40800001
Stop Timer 800F40900001
Upside Down Mode 800F40610001
Flat Cars 800F40B10001
Fat Cars 800F40B10002
Giant Cars 800F40B10003

STAR FOX 64
Hyper Laser 8015791B0002
Infinite Armor 8013AB2700FF
Infinite Armor 80137C4700FF
Loads O' Hits 8015790B00FF
Unlimited Lives P1 .801579110040
Unlimited Smart Bombs P1 . . . . .8016DC130004

STAR FOX VERSION 1.1
Infinite Smart Bombs P1 . . . . .80177DA30004
Infinite Lives P1 . . . . .80161AA10003

STAR WARS SHADOWS OF THE EMPIRE
Unlimited Lives 800E05CB00FF
Unlimited Missiles 800E126500FF

STAR WARS SHADOWS OF THE EMPIRE VERSION 1.1
Unlimited Lives 800E0EB300FF
Unlimited Missiles 800E1B5500FF

SUB ZERO: MORTAL KOMBAT MYTHOLOGIES
Infinite Lives 8010BCFF0005

TOP GEAR RALLY
Extra Tracks 813243CEFFFF
Extra Vehicles 813243CCFFFF
Level 1 Points 8032431F0064
Level 2 Points 803243210064
Level 3 Points 803243230064
Level 4 Points 803243250064
Level 5 Points 803243270064
Level 6 Points 803243290064

WAR GODS
Unlimited Time 8033F31B0063
Cheat Menu 803365930001

WAVE RACE
Infinite Time Stunt Mode..............801C295E00FF
Misses Don't Count 801C27CF0000
Only Play Glacier Coast 800DA7530007
Super Speed 801C27C70050
Maximum Power 801C27C70005
R Shoulder Turbo Boost 801C27C70005
R Shoulder Turbo Boost D01540510010
R Shoulder Turbo Boost 801C27C70020
Infinite Course Out Time 801C298300FF
99 Points 801CB0A30063

WCW VS. NWO
Infinite Time 800F16EF0000
Extra Characters 8006066500FF
Maximum Spirit P1 ....800F08010064
No Spirit P1 ....800F08010000
Maximum Spirit P2 ....800F0BA10064
No Spirit P2 ....800F0BA10000

WHEEL OF FORTUNE
Extra Cash P1 ....810B9992FFFF

8

PlayStation

A-TRAIN
Infinite Money. 800a62309400
Infinite Money. 800a62327735

ACE COMBAT 2
Extra Planes 80010C440101
Extra Planes 80010C460101
Extra Planes 80010C480101
Extra Planes 80010C4A0101
Extra Planes 80010C4C0101
Extra Planes 80010C4E0101
Extra Planes 80010C500101
Extra Planes 80010C520101
Infinite Fuel. 8003936C2400
Infinite Fuel. 8003936E82AC
Infinite Missiles 8002CAA80000
Infinite Missiles 8002CAAA0000

ADIDAS POWER SOCCER
Team A Scores 0 . . . . 800DAC4E0000
Team B Scores 0 . . . . 800DAC500000

ADVENTURES OF LOMAX
Always Have Helmet 8006B714FFFF
Always Have Helmet 8006B71CFFFF
Infinite Bridges 8006B6600009
Infinite Credits 8006B7E00009
Infinite Digging 8006B8B40009
Infinite Flames 8006B8C80009
Infinite Lives 8006B8540063

AGILE WARRIOR
Infinite AMRAAM 80060F360064
Infinite B61SRAM 80060F340064
Infinite Bunkerbusters 80060F2A0064
Infinite Cluster Bombs 80060F300064
Infinite Fuel Air Explosives 80060F320064
Infinite Mavericks 80060F2E0064
Infinite Napalm 80060F2C0064
Infinite Rockets 80060F280064
Infinite Sidewinders 80060F260064

AIR COMBAT
Unlimited Fuels 800EEB008FFF
Unlimited Missiles 800EEB0C0040

ALIEN TRILOGY
Have Flame Thrower 8008F34A0029
Have Pulse Rifle 8008F3420029
Have Shotgun 8008F33E0029
Have Smartgun 8008F3460029
Infinite Batteries 8009A05A03E7
Infinite Bullets 8009A04603E7
Infinite Charges 8009A05803E7
Infinite Flame Fuel 8009A05203E7
Infinite Health 8009A04003E7
Infinite Pulse Ammo .8009A04C03E7
Infinite Shotgun Shells 8009A04A03E7
Infinite Smartgun Ammo 8009A05403E7
Rapid Fire 8009A0240001

ALL STAR BASEBALL '97
Away Team Wins 800439681900
Home Team Wins 800439680019

ALLIED GENERAL
Infinite Prestige 800F0ACCFFFF

ALUNDRA
Infinite Health. 801AC4AC0032
Infinite Health. 801AC4B00032
Infinite Gilder 801DD5C4270F
Infinite Magic. 801DD5C00004
Infinite Magic. 801DD5C20004
99 Keys. 801DD6C40063
Legend Sword. 801DD5F00001

Steel Flail **801DD5F80001**
Ice Wand. **801DD6080001**
Fire Wand **801DD6100001**
Earth Book **801DD6800001**
Water Book **801DD6880001**
Fire Book **801DD6900001**
Wind Book. **801DD6980001**

ANDRETTI RACING
Infinite Fuel 801EB3A83CF8
Infinite Fuel 801ECA8C3732
Infinite Fuel 801E01940040
Infinite Fuel 801E019C0040
Qualify in 1st 801E35CA036D
Qualify in 1st 801EB360C9AE
Qualify in 1st 801EB3740111

ARCADE'S GREATEST HITS ATARI COLLECTION
Infinite Ships (Asteroids) 800F595A0303
Infinite Tanks (Battlezone) 80132E4C0003
Infinite Lives (Centipede) 8011A93C0203
Infinite Lives (Tempest) 801250800003

AREA 51
Auto-Reload P1 . . . . .8006D0340008
Auto-Reload P2 . . . . .8006D0E00008
Infinite Grenades P1 . . . . .8006D0380001
Infinite Grenades P2 . . . . .8006D0E40001
Infinite Health P1 . . . . .8006D0600004
Infinite Health P2 . . . . .8006D10C0004

ARMORED CORE
Infinite Armor. 801A28188000
Infinite Energy. 80040FBE6D60
Infinite Money. 80039CA600FF
Left Shoulder Weapon Ammo 800412C60028
Right Arm Weapon Ammo 8004128A01F4
Right Shoulder Weapon Ammo 800413020028

BATMAN FOREVER
Infinite Health P1 . . . . .800E2EDC0014

11

BATTLE ARENA TOSHINDEN

Infinite Health P1	.801BC1880000
Infinite Time	.801CA6E80B3A
Select Gaia	.801BC11A0008
Select Sho	.801BC11A0009

BATTLE ARENA TOSHINDEN 3

Extra Characters	.801B27B00001
Extra Characters	.801B27AA0001

BATTLESPORT

Infinite Health P1	.801FCA420064
Infinite Health P2	.801FCAD60064

BATTLESTATIONS

Infinite Health P1	.800C368C0064
Infinite Health P2	.800C39BC0064

BEASTWARS

Start Button for Health Restore	D00D4E3C0020
Start Button for Health Restore	800D33DC1518

BEYOND THE BEYOND

Infinite Cash	.80103884FFFF
Infinite Health (Annie)	.80114A5C03E7
Infinite Health (Annie)	.80114A5E03E7
Infinite Health (Percy)	.80114AE403E7
Infinite Health (Percy)	.80114AE603E7
Infinite Health (Samson)	.80114B6C03E7
Infinite Health (Samson)	.80114B6E03E7
Infinite Health (Tont)	.80114C7C03E7
Infinite Health (Tont)	.80114C7E03E7
Infinite Health P1	.801149D403E7
Infinite Health P1	.801149D603E7

Infinite LP (Annie) 80114A5403E7
Infinite LP (Annie) 80114A5603E7
Infinite LP (Edward) 80114BEC03E7
Infinite LP (Edward) 80114BEE03E7
Infinite LP (Percy) 80114ADC03E7
Infinite LP (Percy) 80114ADE03E7
Infinite LP (Samson) 80114B6403E7
Infinite LP (Samson) 80114B6603E7
Infinite LP (Tont) 80114C7403E7
Infinite LP (Tont) 80114C7603E7
Infinite LP P1 . . . . .801149CC03E7
Infinite LP P1 . . . . .801149CE03E7
Infinite MP (Annie) 80114A5803E7
Infinite MP (Annie) 80114A5A03E7
Infinite MP (Edward) 80114BF003E7
Infinite MP (Edward) 80114BF203E7
Infinite MP (Percy) 80114AE003E7
Infinite MP (Percy) 80114AE203E7
Infinite MP (Samson) .80114B6803E7
Infinite MP (Samson) .80114B6A03E7
Infinite MP (Tont) 80114C7803E7
Infinite MP (Tont) 80114C7A03E7
Infinite MP P1 . . . . .801149D003E7
Infinite MP P1 . . . . .801149D203E7
Quick Level Gain (Annie) 80114A78FFFF
Quick Level Gain (Percy) 80114B00FFFF
Quick Level Gain (Samson) 80114B88FFFF
Quick Level Gain (Tont) 80114C98FFFF
Quick Level Gain P1 . . . . .801149F0FFFF
Super Attack (Annie) 80114A6003E7
Super Attack (Edward) .80114BF803E7
Super Attack (Percy) 80114AE803E7
Super Attack (Samson) .80114B7003E7
Super Attack (Tont) 80114C8003E7
Super Attack P1 . . . . .801149D803E7
Super Defense (Annie) .80114A6403E7
Super Defense (Annie) .80114A6603E7
Super Defense (Edward) 80114BFC03E7
Super Defense (Edward) 80114BFE03E7
Super Defense (Percy) .80114AEC03E7
Super Defense (Percy) .80114AEE03E7
Super Defense (Samson) 80114B7403E7
Super Defense (Samson) 80114B7603E7

Super Defense (Tont)	.80114C8403E7
Super Defense (Tont)	.80114C8603E7
Super Defense P1	.801149DC03E7
Super Defense P1	.801149DE03E7
Super IQ (Annie)	.80114A6C03E7
Super IQ (Edward)	.80114C0603E7
Super IQ (Percy)	.80114AF603E7
Super IQ (Samson)	.80114B7E03E7
Super IQ (Tont)	.80114C8E03E7
Super IQ P1	.801149E603E7
Super Luck (Annie)	.80114A7003E7
Super Luck (Edward)	.80114C0A03E7
Super Luck (Percy)	.80114AFA03E7
Super Luck (Samson)	.80114B8203E7
Super Luck (Tont)	.80114C9203E7
Super Luck P1	.801149EA03E7
Super Speed (Annie)	.80114A6803E7
Super Speed (Annie)	.80114A6A03E7
Super Speed (Edward)	.80114C0003E7
Super Speed (Edward)	.80114C0203E7
Super Speed (Percy)	.80114AF003E7
Super Speed (Percy)	.80114AF203E7
Super Speed (Samson)	.80114B7803E7
Super Speed (Samson)	.80114B7A03E7
Super Speed (Tont)	.80114C8803E7
Super Speed (Tont)	.80114C8A03E7
Super Speed P1	.801149E003E7
Super Speed P1	.801149E203E7
Super Strength (Annie)	.80114A6203E7
Super Strength (Edward)	.80114BFA03E7
Super Strength (Percy)	.80114AEA03E7
Super Strength (Samson)	.80114B7203E7
Super Strength (Tont)	.80114C8203E7
Super Strength P1	.801149DA03E7

BIG BASS WORLD CHAMPIONSHIP

Infinite Bright Lures	.8004D2780000
Infinite Bright Lures	.8004D27A0000
Infinite Natural Lures	.8004D2640000
Infinite Natural Lures	.8004D2660000

BIG HURT BASEBALL
Team I Scores 15 .... .80173BD8000F

BLACK DAWN
Infinite Missiles .... .8005FCF00064
Infinite Napalm .... .8005FCF403E7
Infinite Rockets .... .8005FCF20064
Infinite TAC .... .8005FCF603E7

BOGEV DEAD 6
Infinite AMRAAM Missiles .... .800BC6860064
Infinite Armor .... .801B9FDC0964
Infinite Credits .... .801C29C20005
Infinite Fuel .... .800817122F61
Infinite Fuel .... .801C21702F61
Infinite HARM Missiles .... .800BC6880064
Infinite Maverick Missiles .... .800BC68A0064
Infinite Sidewinders .... .800BC6840064
Infinite Time .... .80080B2403E7

BRAHMA FORCE

Breaker Mortar	800E0CA6FFFF
Dual Buster and Mobs	800E0CA4FFFF
Hasler 1000 and 3000 Rifles	800E0C98FFFF
Hensolt and Triple Barrel	800E0C9AFFFF
Hydra Laser	800E0CA2FFFF
Infinite Bombs	800E0C7C03E8
Infinite Bullets	800E0C7403E8
Infinite Durability	800E0C6403E8
Infinite Durability	800E0C6603E8
Infinite Laser Energy	800E0D2A06B0
Infinite Missiles	800E0C7803E8
Infinite Mortar Shells	800E0C7A03E8
MIV Mortar	800E0CA8FFFF
Never Overheat	800E0A6E0000
Polar Ray and Synwave	800E0CA0FFFF
Prokian and Hadron Lasers	800E0C9EFFFF
Rapid Fire Rifle	800E0C9CFFFF

BROKEN HELIX

Alien Weapon	8006FE68011E
Amplifier	8006FE40010A
C-4 Explosive	8006FE780126
Detonator 1	8006FE560115
Energy Armor	8006FE5A0117
Energy Pack	8006FE4A010F
First Aid	8006FE2E0101
Flame Thrower	8006FE64011C
Force Field Device	8006FE5E0119
Gas Card	8006FE4C0110
Grenades	8006FE760125
Helix Files 1	8006FE540114
Infinite Armor	8005C9180064
Jewel 1	8006FE4E0111
Key 1	8006FE340104
Key 10	8006FE740124
Key 2	8006FE360105
Key 3	8006FE380106
Key 4	8006FE60011A
Key 5	8006FE3C0108
Key 6	8006FE3E0109
Key 7	8006FE6E0121
Key 8	8006FE700122
Key 9	8006FE720123

Large Energy	.8006FE300102
Lift Key I	.8006FE3A0107
Missile	.8006FE66011D
Orders I	.8006FE580116
Organic Attachment	.8006FE6A011F
Password I	.8006FE520113
Photo	.8006FE42010B
Plasma	.8006FE6C0120
Rapid Fire	.8006FE62011B
Save	.8006FE44010C
Virus Antidote	.8006FE48010E
Wire Cutters	.8006FE500112

BUGRIDERS
Infinite Time	800C84D40015

BUBBLE BOBBLE
Infinite Lives (Bubble Bobble)	.80176AC80002
Infinite Lives (Rainbow Islands)	.8005DC3A0003

BUSHIDO BLADE
Automatic Win	8013D6360001
Automatic Win	8013D5240005
Enable All Endings	800A10D4FFFF
Enable All Endings	800A10D8FFFF
Enable Katze VS. Mode	800A10040001
Hold L2 Heart Attack Button	D013D1D80001
Hold L2 Heart Attack Button	8013D5240005

BUSTER BROS. COLLECTION
Infinite Lives (Buddies)	.801712260202
Infinite Lives (Buster)	.800C59400003
Infinite Lives (Super Buster)	.800A4A100003

CASPER
Brass Key	.8007EA2C0001
Infinite Health	.8007F01C0064
Infinite Health	.8007F02C0064
Infinite Health	.801FBD800064
Iron Key	.8007EA280001

17

CASTLEVANIA
Infinite Gold 80097BF0FFFF
Infinite Hearts. 80097BA80063
Infinite HP. 80097BA003E7
Infinite MP 80097BB003E7
Quick Level Gain 80097BECFFFF

COLLEGE SLAM
Infinite Boost P1 . . . . .80078208002F
Infinite Boost P2 . . . . .80078528002F
Team 1 Scores 999 . . . . .8006551003E7
Team 2 Never Scores 800655200000

COLONY WARS
Infinite Shields. 800463B400C8
Energy Weapon Never Overheats. 80119C4C0000
Energy Weapon Never Overheats. 80119C800000
Energy Weapon Never Overheats. 80119CB40000
Energy Weapon Never Overheats. 80119CE80000
Energy Weapon Never Overheats. 80119D1C0000
Infinite Missiles First Position 80119CC00001
Infinite Missiles Second Position 80119CF40001
Infinite Missiles Third Position. 80119D280001
Infinite Missiles Fourth Position 80119D5C0001

COMMAND & CONQUER
Infinite Funds 8011B964FFFF
Infinite Funds 8011C04CFFFF

COMMAND & CONQUER: RED ALERT
Infinite Funds (1). 801046D00000
Infinite Funds (2). 801046D20000

CONTRA
Infinite Health P1 . . . . 800DC7840009

COOLBOARDERS

All Awards	801EF97C000F
All Awards	801EFAB8000F
All Awards	801EFBF4000F
All Awards	801EFD30000F
All Awards	801EFE6C000F
Camera Angle 1	8018EF3001A0
Extra Tracks	801EF82A0005
High Scoring	800162100001
High Scoring	800162120001
High Stability	801827A40000
Score Sheet	8005D0C6FFFF
Score Sheet	8005D1D2FFFF
Snowman and Extra Boards	801EF82E0017
Tiny Boarder	8018EF280F00

CRASH BANDICOOT

Level Select	800619480020
Master Code	D005C89C0014

CRASH BANDICOOT 2

100 Lives	8006CBD06400
All Crystals	8006CDA4FFFF
All Crystals	8006CDA6FFFF
All Crystals	8006CDA8FFFF
All Gems	8006CC28FFFF
All Gems	8006CC2AFFFF
All Gems	8006CC2CFFFF
All Gems	8006CC2EFFFF

CRITICAL DEPTH

Infinite Health P1	801DF15E0073
Infinite Slow Poke/Remote Charges	801DF5D40909
Infinite Shaker/Pilot Torpedoes	801DF5D20909
Infinite Neato Torpedoes/Piranha Swarms	801DF5D00909
Infinite Magnetic Suckers	801DF5CE0900

CRITICOM

Infinite Health P1	80059de80300
Infinite Health P1	80059f580320
Infinite Health P1	8005a0c80320
Infinite Health P2	80059c780320
Infinite Health P2	80059b080320
Infinite Health P2	80059de80300
Master Code	d005a2f27d24

CROC

5 Crystals	80074AC8001F
6 Gobbos Saved	8007496C0006
Infinite Crystals	800749640064
Infinite Lives	80074FDC0003
Jigsaw Pieces	80074E6C0008
Silver Key	80074AC40001

CROW

Infinite Health	80087862007F
Infinite Health	8008313AB712

CRYPT KILLER

Infinite Bombs P1	800FC17A0009
Infinite Bombs P2	800FC1D60009
Infinite Health P1	800FC1740005
Infinite Health P2	800FC1D00005
P1 Has Automatic	800FC1780004
P1 Has Grenade Launcher	800FC1780002
P1 Has Machine Gun	800FC1780003
P1 Has Shotgun	800FC1780001
P2 Has Automatic	800FC1D40004
P2 Has Grenade Launcher	800FC1D40002
P2 Has Machine Gun	800FC1D40003
P2 Has Shotgun	800FC1D40001

CYBERSLED

Infinite Missiles	8014A6480005
Infinite Shields	8014A6621000

D

Infinite Mirror Hints	800718E40303
Infinite Mirror Hints	801324B40001
Infinite Time	80053AE0BEDE
Infinite Time	80053B24BEDE

Infinite Time	800689B8BFCE
Infinite Time	80071120044E
Infinite Time	8010C484020C

DARK FORCES

Assault Cannon	800950B2FFFF
Assault Cannon Ammo	8009511203E7
Auto-Gun	800950A2FFFF
Blue Key	800950BEFFFF
Infinite Blaster Ammo	8009510803E7
Infinite Cells	8009510C03E7
Infinite Health	8009512C0064
Infinite Mines	8009511C03E7
Infinite Shells	8009511A03E7
Infinite Shields	800951280064
Infinite Thermal Detonators	8009511403E7
Jeron Fusion Cutter	800950AAFFFF
Laser Rifle	8009509CFFFF
Level Select	80010018000F
Packered Mortar Gun	800950A6FFFF
Red Key	800950B6FFFF
Stouker Concussion Rifle	800950AEFFFF
Yellow Key	800950BAFFFF

DARKLIGHT CONFLICT

| High Durability | 8010E5640000 |
| Infinite Energy | 800870281E00 |

DARKSTALKERS

| Infinite Health P1 | 800CD1A00090 |
| Infinite Health P2 | 800CD5140090 |

DEFCON 5

| Infinite Ammo | 800D53AC0014 |
| Infinite Health | 800E7C300064 |

DESCENT

Infinite Concussion Missiles	800D10BA0009
Infinite Energy	800D10A20064
Infinite Homing Missiles	800D10BC0009
Infinite Proximity Bombs	800D10BE0009
Infinite Shields	800D10A60064

DESCENT MAXIMUM

Always Have Earth Shakers	800E933A0063
Always Have Earth Shakers	800F86680009
Extra Weapons	800E930CFFFF
Infinite Energy	800E92FE03E7
Infinite Lives	800E93040404
Infinite Shields	800E930203E7
Infinite Vulcan Ammo	800E9316270F
Level 5 Laser	800E93060404

DESTRUCTION DERBY 2

Enable All Arenas	8007975C0004
Enable All Tracks	800797580007
Infinite Armor	8008A3440000
Infinite Armor	8008A34C0000
Infinite Armor	8008A3540000
Infinite Armor	8008A3580000
Infinite Armor	8008A3600000
Infinite Armor	8008A3680000
Score 1000 Points	8009569203E7

DISNEY'S HERCULES

Helmet of Invincibilty	80034DC400C8
Infinite Energy	80034DBC0080
Infinite Fireball Sword	80034DC000C8
Infinite Lightning Sword	80034DBE00C8
Infinite Lives	30034DA40009
Infinite Sonic Sword	80034DC200C8

DISRUPTOR

18mm Ammo	80056A9403E7
18mm Auto	800770FE0001
AM Blaster	8007710C0001
AM Cyclone	800771100001
Infinite Health	8007766003E7
Lock-on Cannon	800771080001
Phase Ammo	80056A9803E7
Phase Repeater	800771040001
Phase Rifle	800771000001
Plasma	800771180001
Rapid Fire	800776800000
Zodiac	800771140001

DOOM

Have BFG	800A865C0001
Have Blue Key	800A86180001
Have Chaingun	800A86500001
Have Chainsaw	800A86600001
Have Double-Barrel Shotgun	800A864C0001
Have Map	800A860C0001
Have Plasma Rifle	800A86580001
Have Red Key	800A86140001
Have Rocket Launcher	800A86540001
Have Shotgun	800A86480001
Have Yellow Key	800A861C0001
Invincible	800A85FC0001
Invincible	800A85F40001
Invincible	800A85F00064
Mega Rapid Fire	800A86C00001
Unlimited Bullets	800A86640064
Unlimited Plasma	800A866C0064
Unlimited Rockets	800A86700064
Unlimited Shotgun Shells	800A86680064

DOOM VERSION 1.1

Have BFG	800A887C0001
Have Blue Key	800A88380001
Have Chaingun	800A88700001
Have Chainsaw	800A88800001
Have Double-Barrel Shotgun	800A886C0001
Have Map	800A882C0001
Have Plasma Rifle	800A88780001
Have Red Key	800A88340001
Have Rocket Launcher	800A88740001
Have Shotgun	800A88680001
Have Yellow Key	800A883C0001
Invincible	800A881C0001
Invincible	800A88140001
Invincible	800A88100064
Mega Rapid Fire	800A88E00001
Unlimited Bullets	800A88840064
Unlimited Plasma	800A888C0064
Unlimited Rockets	800A88900064
Unlimited Shotgun Shells	800A88880064

DRAGON BALL GT

Infinite Health P1	800728400188
Infinite Power P1	8007284200C4
Infinite Health P2	800728BC0188
Infinite Power P2	800728BE00C4
No Health P1	800728400000
No Power P1	800728420000
No Health P2	800728BC0000
No Power P2	800728BE0000

DUKE NUKEM

Infinite Pistol Ammo	800EC93C00C8
Infinite Shotgun Shells	800EC93E0032
Infinite Chaingun Ammo	800EC94000C8
Infinite RPG Rockets	800EC9420032
Infinite Pipe Bombs	800EC9440032
Infinite Shrink Ray Ammo	800EC9460032
Infinite Devastator Ammo	800EC9480063
Infinite Freezer Ammo	800EC94C0063
Shotgun	800ECA1A0101
Have Chaingun/RPG	800ECA1C0101
Have Pipe Bombs/Shrink Ray	800ECA1E0101
Have Devastator/Freezer	800ECA200101

DYNASTY WARRIORS

Infinite Health P1	800B2CDC00C8
Infinite Health P2	800B364C00C8

EPIDEMIC

Infinite Brain Destructors	800A7EB403E7
Infinite EP	800A7E5403E8
Infinite Erosion Missiles	800A7EB203E7
Infinite Float Mines	800A7EB603E7
Infinite HP	800A7E5203E8
Infinite Machinegun Ammo	800A7EA603E7
Infinite Napalm	800A7EB003E7
Infinite SP	800A7E5603E8
Infinite Splasher Arrows	800A7EAE03E7
Infinite Veda Missiles	800A7EAC03E7
Lasers Never Overheat	800A7E9400C8

EXCALIBUR

Infinite Health	801222E81000

EXTREME GAMES

Infinite Health	8007A2700500

FANTASTIC FOUR

Infinite Health P1	800E038C0042
Infinite Health P1	800E038E0042
Infinite Health P2	800E058C0042
Infinite Health P2	800E058E0042
Infinite Lives P1	800BA1700309

FELONY 11-79

Bus	80070B9C0001
CIV	80070B900001
Diablo	80070BBC0001
DTK	80070BA00001
ELS	80070BC40001
Formula 1	80070BAC0001
Garbage Truck	80070BD40001
GT1	80070BB80001
GT5	80070B880001
Infinite Damage	8009AE640000
Infinite Time	800A34180001
Infinite Time	801FFAFC02BE
Infinite Time	8009ACF00001

Invisible Vehicle	800A2DDC9B47
Invisible Vehicle	800A2DEC59E2
Limo	80070B940001
NSR	80070B840001
PCS	80070BB40001
PLC	80070BB00001
RC Car	80070BD80001
Score 0 Points	8009AE080000
Score 0 Points	8009AE0A0000
Score Millions	8009AE080000
Score Millions	8009AE0A00FF
Street Sweeper	80070BD00001
Tank	80070BC80001
Viper	80070BC00001
VW	80070BCC0001

FIFA '96

Infinite Time	80016CC00000
Player 1 Always Scores 10	80016CD2000A
Player 2 Always Scores	80016CD40000

FIGHTING FORCE

Load o' Special Attacks P1+P2	D0093A16FFFF
Load o' Special Attacks P1+P2	80024F3C0000
Load o' Special Attacks P1+P2	80024F3E0000
Infinite Credits	80093D500009

FINAL DOOM

BFG 9000	800AB39C0001
Blue Key	800AB3580001
Chaingun	800AB3900001
Chainsaw	800AB3A00001
Infinite Armor	800AB3340064
Infinite Bullets	800AB3A403E7
Infinite Plasma	800AB3AC03E7
Infinite Rockets	800AB3B003E7
Infinite Shotgun Shells	800AB3A803E7
Map	800AB34C0001
Plasma Rifle	800AB3980001
Rapid Fire	800AB3F80001
Red Key	800AB3540001
Rocket Launcher	800AB3940001
Shotgun	800AB3880001
Super Shotgun	800AB38C0001
Yellow Key	800AB35C0001

FINAL FANTASY VII

Infinite Gil	8009D260FFFF
Quick Level Gain	8009D7D8FFFF

FINAL FANTASY TACTICS

Infinite Gil.	800577CE0FFF
Infinite HP Character 1	801924F403E7
Infinite HP Character 1	801924F603E7
Infinite MP Character 1	801924F803E7
Infinite MP Character 1	801924FA03E7
CT Full Character 1	801924FC0064
Infinite HP Character 2.	801926B403E7
Infinite HP Character 2.	801926B603E7
Infinite MP Character 2	801926B803E7
Infinite MP Character 2	801926BA03E7
CT Full Character 2	801926BC0064
Infinite HP Character 3.	8019287403E7
Infinite HP Character 3.	8019287603E7
Infinite MP Character 3	8019287803E7
Infinite MP Character 3	801928 7A03E7
CT Full Character 3	8019287C0064
Infinite HP Character 4.	80192A3403E7
Infinite HP Character 4.	80192A3603E7
Infinite MP Character 4	80192A3803E7
Infinite MP Character 4	80192A3A03E7
CT Full Character 4	80192A3C0064
Infinite HP Character 5.	80192BF403E7
Infinite HP Character 5.	80192BF603E7
Infinite MP Character 5	80192BF803E7
Infinite MP Character 5	80192BFA03E7
CT Full Character 5	80192BFC0064

FORMULA 1

Buggy Mode	8009DC020001
French Mode	8009DC080001
Lava Mode	8009DC040001
Spanish Mode	8009DC0A0001

FORMULA 1 CHAMPIONSHIP EDITION

Infinite Time	800B34400C60
Select Button For Turbo	D00BCEA80001
Select Button For Turbo	800C6F507000

FROGGER

Infinite Lives	800B6C500009
Infinite Time	800B3DF80900

FULL CONTACT

Away Team Scores 0	8008AB360000
Home Team Scores 0	8008AB340000

G POLICE
Infinite Cluster Bombs	800F5CBC0063
Infinite Firestreak Missiles	800F5CB00063
Infinite Hyper Missiles	800F5CAC0063
Infinite Rockets	800F5CB80063
Infinite Starburst Missiles	800F5CB40063

GAMEBREAKER FOOTBALL
Away Team Scores 0	800B17440000
Home Team Scores 0	800B17400000

GAMEDAY '98
Away Team Scores 0	800F47C80000
Home Team Scores 0	800F47C40000

GEX
Infinite Lives	80097B2C0064
Infinite Health	80097B1C0003

GHOST IN THE SHELL
Have All Movies	801127360001
Have All Movies	801127380001
Have All Movies	8011273A0001
Have All Movies	8011273C0001
Have All Movies	8011273E0001
Have All Movies	801127400001
Have All Movies	801127420001
Have All Movies	801127440001
Have All Movies	801127460001
Have All Movies	801127480001
Have All Movies	8011274A0001
Have All Movies	8011274C0001
Have All Movies	8011274E0001
Have All Movies	801127500001
Have All Movies	801127520001
Have All Movies	801127540001

GOAL STORM
Team 1 Scores 9	301617300009
Team 2 Scores 0	301617310000

GOLDEN NUGGET
Infinite Cash	D000857C00FF
Infinite Cash	801E26A2FFFF

GRAND SLAM
Away Team Scores 100	800F59000064
Home Team Scores 100	800F5C580064

GRAND TOUR RACING '98

Easter Island Levels (Ahmed) 800269360007
Easter Island Levels (Baptiste) 8002698A0007
Easter Island Levels (Ivanov) 8002697E0007
Easter Island Levels (Lumiere) 800269660007
Easter Island Levels (Morgen) 800269420007
Easter Island Levels (Roberts) 800269720007
Easter Island Levels (Rossi) 8002694E0007
Easter Island Levels (Xu) 8002695A0007
Egypt Levels (Ahmed) 8002693E0007
Egypt Levels (Baptiste) 800269920007
Egypt Levels (Ivanov) 800269860007
Egypt Levels (Lumiere) 8002696E0007
Egypt Levels (Morgen) 8002694A0007
Egypt Levels (Roberts) 8002697A0007
Egypt Levels (Rossi) 800269560007
Egypt Levels (Xu) 800269620007
Hong Kong Levels (Ahmed) 8002693C0007
Hong Kong Levels (Baptiste) 800269900007
Hong Kong Levels (Ivanov) 800269840007
Hong Kong Levels (Lumiere) 8002696C0007
Hong Kong Levels (Morgen) 800269480007
Hong Kong Levels (Roberts) 800269780007
Hong Kong Levels (Rossi) 800269540007
Hong Kong Levels (Xu) 800269600007
Moscow Levels (Ahmed) 800269340007
Moscow Levels (Baptiste) 800269880007
Moscow Levels (Ivanov) 8002697C0007
Moscow Levels (Lumiere) 800269640007
Moscow Levels (Morgen) 800269400007
Moscow Levels (Roberts) 800269700007
Moscow Levels (Rossi) 8002694C0007
Moscow Levels (Xu) 800269580007
Scotland Levels (Amhed) 8002693A0007
Scotland Levels (Baptiste) 8002698E0007
Scotland Levels (Ivanov) 800269820007
Scotland Levels (Lumiere) 8002696A0007
Scotland Levels (Morgen) 800269460007
Scotland Levels (Roberts) 800269760007
Scotland Levels (Rossi) 800269520007
Scotland Levels (Xu) 8002695E0007
Switzerland Levels (Ahmed) 800269380007
Switzerland Levels (Baptiste) 8002698C0007
Switzerland Levels (Ivanov) 800269800007
Switzerland Levels (Lumiere) 800269680007
Switzerland Levels (Morgen) 800269440007
Switzerland Levels (Roberts) 800269740007
Switzerland Levels (Rossi) 800269500007
Switzerland Levels (Xu) 8002695C0007

GUNSHIP

Infinite Ammo 800A429803E7
Infinite Ammo 800A429A03E7
Infinite Ammo 800A429C03E7
Infinite Ammo 800A429E03E7
Infinite Fuel 800A42AA0064

HERC'S ADVENTURES

Infinite Endurance PI 800C4AE400BE
Infinite Endurance PI 800C4AE600BE
Infinite Health PI 800C4AE000BE
Infinite Spears PI 800C4AF60063
Infinite Money PI 800C4AE80063
Ray Gun PI 800C4B06001E
Infinite Lightning Bolts PI 800C4AF00009
Infinite Keys PI 800C4B3A0009
A Key PI 800C4B400001
P Key PI 800C4B420001
D Key PI 800C4B440001
H Key PI 800C4B3C0001
U Key PI 800C4B3E0001

HEXEN

All Keys 800E7DA0FFFF
Extra Weapons 800E7DB40001
Extra Weapons 800E7DB80001
High Armor Class 800E7C7E01E0
Infinite Blue Mana 800E7DC000C8
Infinite Green Mana .800E7DC400C8

HI OCTANE

Infinite Ammo 80160EEC27FF
Infinite Ammo 801614BC27FF
Infinite Ammo 801616AC27FF
Infinite Ammo 801610DC27FF
Infinite Ammo 80160CFC27FF

Infinite Fuel	80160EEA27FF
Infinite Fuel	801614BA27FF
Infinite Fuel	801616AA27FF
Infinite Fuel	801610DA27FF
Infinite Fuel	80160CFA27FF
Infinite Shield	80160EEE27FF
Infinite Shield	801614BE27FF
Infinite Shield	801616AE27FF
Infinite Shield	801610DE27FF
Infinite Shield	80160CFE27FF
Maximum Boost	8015CD060003
Maximum Boost	80158EEA0003
Maximum Boost	801594C60003
Maximum Boost	801570D60003
Maximum Boost	801578420003
Maximum Boost	80138A3A0003
Maximum Boost	801595F20003
Maximum Boost	8015807A0003
Maximum Mini-Gun	8015CDCE0003
Maximum Mini-Gun	80158FB20003
Maximum Mini-Gun	8015958E0003
Maximum Mini-Gun	8015719E0003
Maximum Mini-Gun	8015790A0003
Maximum Mini-Gun	80158B020003
Maximum Mini-Gun	801596BA0003
Maximum Missiles	8015CD6A0003
Maximum Missiles	80158F4E0003
Maximum Missiles	8015952A0003
Maximum Missiles	8015713A0003
Maximum Missiles	801578A60003
Maximum Missiles	80158A9E0003
Maximum Missiles	801596560003
Maximum Missiles	801590DE0003
Mini-Gun Coolant	8015CDAE0000
Mini-Gun Coolant	80159F920000
Mini-Gun Coolant	8015956E0000
Mini-Gun Coolant	8015717E0000
Mini-Gun Coolant	801578EA0000
Mini-Gun Coolant	80158AE20000
Mini-Gun Coolant	8015969A0000
Mini-Gun Coolant	801591220000
No On-Screen Damage	80160EA00000
No On-Screen Damage	801614700000
No On-Screen Damage	801616600000
No On-Screen Damage	801610900000
No On-Screen Damage	80160CB00000

HIVE
Infinite Shield 8006B5DC1612
Infinite Thrust 800685FC0096

IMPACT RACING
Infinite Ammo 800304F60000
Infinite Ammo 8003032E0000
Infinite Ammo 800302160000
Infinite Ammo 800307E60000
Infinite Ammo 800337720000
Laser Coolant 800B86340000

IN THE HUNT
Infinite Credits P1 . . . . .8007DA680005
Infinite Credits P2 . . . . .8007DA6A0005
Infinite Lives 800DCD480005
Infinite Time 8007D96E0086

INCREDIBLE HULK
Double Damage 800880EC00C6
Infinite Gamma Power 800884040039
Infinite Health 80087D6C0039

JET MOTO
Infinite Turbo 801767000004
Track Select 801766640003

JET MOTO 2
Infinite Turbo (Li'l Dave) 8016BDEE0006
Infinite Turbo (Wild Ride) 8016CD560006
Infinite Turbo (Blade). 8016DCBE0006
Infinite Turbo (Technician). 8016EC260006
Infinite Turbo (The Max) 8016FB8E0006
Infinite Turbo (Vampeera) 80170AF60006
Infinite Turbo (Gadget) 80171A5E0006
Infinite Turbo (Steele) 801729C60006
Infinite Turbo (The Hun) 8017392E0006
Infinite Turbo (Bomber). 801748960006

JOHNNY BAZOOKATONE
Infinite Health 800B5A980005
Infinite Lives 800B5A940009

JUPITER STRIKE

Infinite Shield	800BB3D40064
Infinite Shield	800BB8180064
Laser Always Cool	800BB9500064

K-1 ARENA FIGHTERS

Infinite Credits	800B49D40003
Infinite Health PI	800B44BC03E8
Infinite Health PI	800B44C403E8
Infinite Health P2	800B44C003E8
Infinite Health P2	800B44C803E8
Infinite Stamina PI	800B44B401F4
Infinite Stamina P2	800B44B801F4
Low Health PI	800B44BC0000
Low Health PI	800B44C40000
Low Health P2	800B44C00000
Low Health P2	800B44C80000
Low Stamina PI	800B44B40000
Low Stamina P2	800B44B80000
Master Ishii	80103B540008
Master Ishii	80103B560008
Narcolepsy	800C8B580009
Narcolepsy	800C8B700009

KILEAK

Infinite Energy	800B629403CE
Infinite Shields	800B629803E8
Infinite Wales Ammo	800B62C801EF

KILLING ZONE

Enable Code (Must Be On)	80083F2C00C8
Infinite Health PI	8008F9EC0100
Infinite Health P2	8008F9F00100

KING OF FIGHTERS '95

Infinite Health PI	8008B45400CF
Infinite Health PI	800BCFA000CF
Infinite Health P2	8008B5B800CF
Infinite Health P2	800BCFA200CF
No Health P2	8008B5B80000
No Health P2	800BCFA20000

KING'S FIELD

High Magic Power	.8019943E0064
High Strength	.801994380064
Infinite Hit Points	.8019942600FA
Infinite Hit Points	.8019942800FA
Infinite Magic Points	.8019942A00FA
Infinite Magic Points	.8019942C00FA
Loads Of Gold	.80199440C350
Mega Defense	.801994560064
Mega Defense	.801994580064
Mega Defense	.8019945A0064
Mega Defense	.8019945C0064
Mega Defense	.8019945E0064
Mega Defense	.801994600064
Mega Defense	.801994620064
Mega Defense	.801994640064
Mega Defense	.801994660064
Mega Offense	.801994440064
Mega Offense	.801994460064
Mega Offense	.801994480064
Mega Offense	.8019944A0064
Mega Offense	.8019944C0064
Mega Offense	.8019944E0064
Mega Offense	.801994500064
Mega Offense	.801994520064
Rapid Magic Use	.801994321388
Rapid Weapon Use	.8019942E1388

KING'S FIELD II

Infinite Gold	.801B2534FFFF
Infinite HP	.801B24FA03E7
Infinite HP	.801B24FC03E7
Infinite MP	.801B24FE03E7
Infinite MP	.801B250003E7
Magic Meter	.801B25061388
Magic Meter	.801E103AFF00
Magic Meter	.801E1044FF00
Quick Level Gain	.801B24E4FFFF
Strength Meter	.801A120C1208
Strength Meter	.801A120E001A
Strength Meter	.801B25021388
Strength Meter	.801B259C0000
Strength Meter	.801B259E0000

KRAZY IVAN

Infinite 50mm	8008D1A403E7
Infinite Cannon	8008D1B003E7
Infinite Cerebus Missiles	8008D1E00064
Infinite EM Pulse	8008D1C00009
Infinite Hyena Missiles	8008D1D80064
Infinite Kraken	8008D1C40009
Infinite Labor	8008D1A803E7
Infinite Medusa	8008D1C80009
Infinite Plasma	8008D1AC03E7
Infinite Scythe	8008D1B40009
Infinite ULF Pulse	8008D1BC0009
Infinite Vortex Bombs	8008D1B80009
Never Overheat	800D1CB80000

LOST WORLD JURASSIC PARK

23 Lives	80015FE40000
23 Lives	80015FE60000

MACHINE HEAD

Infinite Armor	800BF66000FD
Infinite Disruptor	800C21880064
Infinite Flame Thrower	800C217400FA
Infinite Grenades	800C21840064
Infinite Io-Storm	800C218C0064
Infinite Photons	800C21800064
Infinite Homing Missiles	800C217C0064

MADDEN NFL '97

Away Team Plays as All 50's And 60's	80080F5A0064
Away Team Plays as All 70's	80080F5A0065
Away Team Plays as All 80's	80080F5A0066
Away Team Plays as All AFC 1995	80080F5A0067
Away Team Plays as All Madden All Time	80080F5A0063
Away Team Plays as All NFC 1995	80080F5A0068
Away Team Plays as All EA Sports	80080F5A0069
Away Team Plays as All Tiburon	80080F5A006A
Away Team Scores 0	8008A6400000
Away Team Scores 0	8008D1E80000
Away Team Scores 0	8008A9DC3000
Extra Teams	80080718006B
Home Team Plays as All 50's And 60's	80080F580064
Home Team Plays as All 70's	80080F580065
Home Team Plays as All 80's	80080F580066
Home Team Plays as All AFC 1995	80080F580067
Home Team Plays as All Madden All Time	80080F580063
Home Team Plays as All NFC 1995	80080F580068
Home Team Plays as All EA Sports	80080F580069
Home Team Plays as All Tiburon	80080F58006A
Home Team Scores 0	800886800000
Home Team Scores 0	8008D1E40000
Home Team Scores 0	8008A9D40030

MADDEN NFL '98

Home Team Plays as '60's AFL	8007DD56001E
Home Team Plays as '60 Eagles	8007DD56001F
Home Team Plays as '61 Oilers	8007DD560020
Home Team Plays as '61 Packers	8007DD560021
Home Team Plays as '62 Lions	8007DD560022
Home Team Plays as '62 Giants	8007DD560023
Home Team Plays as '62 Packers	8007DD560024
Home Team Plays as '62 Texans	8007DD560025
Home Team Plays as '63 Bears	8007DD560026
Home Team Plays as '63 Chargers	8007DD560027
Home Team Plays as '64 Colts	8007DD560028
Home Team Plays as '64 Bills	8007DD560029
Home Team Plays as '64 Browns	8007DD56002A
Home Team Plays as '65 Packers	8007DD56002B
Home Team Plays as '65 Bears	8007DD56002C
Home Team Plays as '66 Packers	8007DD56002D

Home Team Plays as '66 Chiefs	8007DD56002E
Home Team Plays as '66 Rams	8007DD56002F
Home Team Plays as '67 Packers	8007DD560030
Home Team Plays as '67 Raiders	8007DD560031
Home Team Plays as '68 Jets	8007DD560032
Home Team Plays as '69 Chiefs	8007DD560033
Home Team Plays as '69 Vikings	8007DD560034
Home Team Plays as '70 Colts	8007DD560035
Home Team Plays as '71 Cowboys	8007DD560036
Home Team Plays as '72 Dolphins	8007DD560037
Home Team Plays as '73 Bills	8007DD560038
Home Team Plays as '73 Dolphins	8007DD560039
Home Team Plays as '74 Steelers	8007DD56003A
Home Team Plays as '75 Steelers	8007DD56003B
Home Team Plays as '75 Cardinals	8007DD56003C
Home Team Plays as '76 Raiders	8007DD56003D
Home Team Plays as '76 Redskins	8007DD56003E
Home Team Plays as '76 Vikings	8007DD56003F
Home Team Plays as '77 Bears	8007DD560040
Home Team Plays as '77 Cowboys	8007DD560041
Home Team Plays as '78 Broncos	8007DD560042
Home Team Plays as '78 Steelers	8007DD560043
Home Team Plays as '79 Steelers	8007DD560044
Home Team Plays as '79 Saints	8007DD560045
Home Team Plays as '79 Rams	8007DD560046
Home Team Plays as '79 Buccaneers	8007DD560047
Home Team Plays as '80 Falcons	8007DD560048
Home Team Plays as '80 Oilers	8007DD560049
Home Team Plays as '80 Raiders	8007DD56004A
Home Team Plays as '80 Eagles	8007DD56004B
Home Team Plays as '81 Bengals	8007DD56004C
Home Team Plays as '81 Chargers	8007DD56004D
Home Team Plays as '81 49ers	8007DD56004E
Home Team Plays as '82 Redskins	8007DD56004F
Home Team Plays as '83 Raiders	8007DD560050
Home Team Plays as '83 Seahawks	8007DD560051
Home Team Plays as '84 Dolphins	8007DD560052
Home Team Plays as '84 49ers	8007DD560053
Home Team Plays as '84 Rams	8007DD560054
Home Team Plays as '84 Cardinals	8007DD560055
Home Team Plays as '85 Bears	8007DD560056
Home Team Plays as '85 Browns	8007DD560057
Home Team Plays as '85 Jets	8007DD560058
Home Team Plays as '85 Patriots	8007DD560059
Home Team Plays as '86 Broncos	8007DD56005A
Home Team Plays as '86 Giants	8007DD56005B
Home Team Plays as '87 Saints	8007DD56005C
Home Team Plays as '87 Redskins	8007DD56005D
Home Team Plays as '88 Bengals	8007DD56005E

Home Team Plays as '88 49ers	8007DD56005F
Home Team Plays as '89 Broncos	8007DD560060
Home Team Plays as '89 49ers	8007DD560061
Home Team Plays as '90 Chiefs	8007DD560062
Home Team Plays as '90 Bills	8007DD560063
Home Team Plays as '90 Raiders	8007DD560064
Home Team Plays as '90 Giants	8007DD560065
Home Team Plays as '90 Eagles	8007DD560066
Home Team Plays as '91 Redskins	8007DD560067
Home Team Plays as '92 Cowboys	8007DD560068
Home Team Plays as '93 Chiefs	8007DD560069
Home Team Plays as '93 Cowboys	8007DD56006A
Home Team Plays as '94 Dolphins	8007DD56006B
Home Team Plays as '94 Lions	8007DD56006C
Home Team Plays as '94 49ers	8007DD56006D
Home Team Plays as '95 Cowboys	8007DD56006E
Home Team Plays as '95 Steelers	8007DD56006F
Home Team Plays as '96 Panthers	8007DD560070
Home Team Plays as '96 Packers	8007DD560071
Home Team Plays as '96 Patriots	8007DD560072
Home Team Plays as AFC	8007DD560073
Home Team Plays as NFC	8007DD560074
Home Team Plays as All 60's	8007DD560075
Home Team Plays as All 70's	8007DD560076
Home Team Plays as All 80's	8007DD560077
Home Team Plays as Madden '97	8007DD560078
Home Team Plays as All Time Madden	8007DD560079
Home Team Plays as All Time Stat Leaders	8007DD56007A
Home Team Plays as EA Sports	8007DD56007B
Home Team Plays as Tiburon	8007DD56007C

MARVEL SUPER HEROES

Infinite Health P1	800919E40080
Infinite Health P1	800921E40090
Infinite Health P2	80091A1C0080
Infinite Health P2	800924140090

MASS DESTRUCTION

Infinite Hi-Explosive Shells	800A8018270F
Infinite Hi-Explosive Shells	800A801A0001
Infinite Mines	800A8024270F
Infinite Mines	800A80260001
Infinite Mortar Shells	800A801E270F
Infinite Mortar Shells	800A80200001
Infinite Torus Bombs	800A802A270F
Infinite Torus Bombs	800A802C0001
Infinite Flame Thrower	800A8030270F
Infinite Flame Thrower	800A80320001

Infinite Guided Missiles	800A8036270F
Infinite Guided Missiles	800A80380001
Infinite Armor	800AC3701F40
Infinite Time	800790D40001

MAXIMUM FORCE

Infinite Credits P1	8006A1300009
Infinite Credits P2	8006A1340009
Infinite Health P1	8006E7F00004
Infinite Health P2	8006E8800004

MDK

Infinite Health	800CB74003E7

MECHWARRIOR 2

Cruise Control	80076CE40400
Infinite Ammo	800D12DE0064
Infinite Ammo	800D12FA0064
Infinite Ammo	800D13160064
Infinite Ammo	800D13320064
Infinite Ammo	800D134E0064
Infinite Ammo	800D136A0064
Infinite Ammo	800D13860064
Infinite Ammo	800D13A20064
Infinite Ammo	800D13BE0064
Infinite Ammo	800D13DA0064
Mystery Super Code	80076CE4FFFF
Never Overheat	800D12680000
Never Overheat	800D126C0000
Speed Increase	800D163C0343

MEGAMAN 8

Astro Crush	801B1ED00001
Flame Sword	801B1EC80001
Flash Bomb	801B1EB40001
Homing Sniper	801B1ECC0001
Ice Wave	801B1EBC0001
Infinite Astro Crush	801B1ED22800

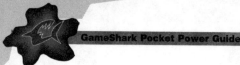

Infinite Flame Swords 801B1ECA2800
Infinite Flash Bombs 801B1EB62800
Infinite Homing Snipers 801B1ECE2800
Infinite Ice Waves 801B1EBE2800
Infinite Mega Balls 801B1EB22800
Infinite Thunder Claws 801B1EBA2800
Infinite Tornadoes 801B1EC22800
Infinite Water Balloons 801B1EC62800
Mega Ball 801B1EB00001
Thunder Claw 801B1EB80001
Tornado Hold 801B1EC00001
Water Balloon 801B1EC40001

MEGAMAN X-4
Infinite Lives 801722040002

MLB '98
Away Team Scores 0 .... 800121F60000
Away Team Scores 50 .... 800121F63232
Home Team Scores 0 .... 800121B40000
Home Team Scores 50 .... 800121B43232

MORTAL KOMBAT
Infinite Energy P1 .... 801CBC3800A6
Infinite Energy P2 .... 801CBC9000A6
Unlimited Time 801EECEC0009

MORTAL KOMBAT TRILOGY
Infinite Health P1 .... 8003219E00A6
Infinite Health P2 .... 8003231600A6
No Health P1 .... 8003219E0000
No Health P2 800323160000

MORTAL KOMBAT TRILOGY VERSION 1.1
Infinite Health P1 .... 8003214600A6
Infinite Health P2 .... 800322BE00A6
No Health P1 800321460000
No Health P2 .... 800322BE0000

MOTOR TOON GRAND PRIX
Extra Characters 800E45740501
Extra Tracks 300E4575000A

Motor Toon GP R 800E45780501
Tank Combat/Submarine X 800E45760501

NAMCO MUSEUM VOL. 1
Infinite Lives Pac-Man 801177EC0003
Infinite Ships Bosconian 8015728C0003

NAMCO MUSEUM VOL. 2
Infinite Lives (Super Pac-Man) 801E10060200
Infinite Lives (Xevious) 80196E480002
Infinite Lives (Xevious) 801DE9BCFF63

NAMCO MUSEUM VOL. 3
Infinite Lives (Dig Dug) 801254180002
Infinite Lives (Galaxian) 8010EC040003
Infinite Lives (Ms. Pac-Man) 801359600002
Infinite Lives (Phozon) 80168D4C0302

NAMCO MUSEUM VOL. 4
Infinite Health (Genji and Heike Clans)......800A01BC3200
Infinite Lives (Ordyne) 800C55C80003
Infinite Lives (Pac-Land) 800580540301

NANOTECH WARRIOR
Infinite Armor 800CAC801000

NASCAR '98
Qualify In 1st 800BF2FC0047

NBA FASTBREAK '98
Home Team Scores 0 ....800EB2300000
Home Team Scores 150 ....800EB2300096
Away Team Scores 150..................800EB2340096
Away Team Scores 0....................800EB2340000
Infinite Creation Points..................8016880C01C2

NBA IN THE ZONE 2
Away Team Scores 0 ....8006ED7E0000
Away Team Scores 0 ....8006ED840000
Home Team Scores 0 ....8007126C0000
Home Team Scores 0 ....8006EBF00000

41

NBA JAM
Other Team Scores 0 ....8007D09C0000

NBA JAM EXTREME
Home Team Scores 0 ....800A227C0000

NBA LIVE '96
Away Team Scores 0 ....8001A55A0000
NBA Home Team Scores 0 ....8001A49E0000

NBA LIVE '98
Away Team Scores 0 ....8007F5780000
Home Team Scores 0 ....8007E1140000
Away Team Scores 150 ....8007F5780096
Home Team Scores 150 ....8007E1140096

NBA SHOOT OUT
Away Team Scores 0 ....80096ED40000
Away Team Scores 0 ....800B4E680000
Home Team Scores 0 ....80096ED00000
Home Team Scores 0 ....8004E6400000

NBA SHOOT OUT '97
Away Team Scores 0 ....800B3E3C0000
Home Team Scores 0 ....800B3E380000
Infinite Creation Points 800D5D3801D8

NCAA FINAL FOUR '97
Away Team Scores 0 ....801EF50C0000
Home Team Scores 0 ....801EE9DC0000

NCAA FOOTBALL '98
Away Team Scores 0 ....800A7FDC0000
Home Team Scores 0 ....800A5E1C0000
Infinite Creation Points 1 ....D00DFDE00032

Infinite Creation Points 1	800DFDDC0000
Infinite Creation Points 2	D00DFDE00032
Infinite Creation Points 2	800DFDDE0000
Infinite Creation Points 3	D00DFDE00032
Infinite Creation Points 3	800E1A640064
Infinite Creation Points 4	D00DFDE00032
Infinite Creation Points 4	800E1A663402
Home Team as Tiburon	8009BF120098
Home Team as '88 West Virginia	8009BF120097
Home Team as '91 Washington	8009BF120096
Home Team as '79 USC	8009BF120095
Home Team as '68 USC	8009BF120094
Home Team as '65 UCLA	8009BF120093
Home Team as '94 Penn State	8009BF120092
Home Team as '86 Penn State	8009BF120091
Home Team as '85 Penn State	8009BF120090
Home Team as '82 Penn State	8009BF12008F
Home Team as '78 Penn State	8009BF12008E
Home Team as '94 Oregon	8009BF12008D
Home Team as '87 Oklahoma	8009BF12008C
Home Team as '85 Oklahoma	8009BF12008B
Home Team as '79 Ohio State	8009BF12008A
Home Team as '68 Ohio State	8009BF120089
Home Team as '89 Notre Dame	8009BF120088
Home Team as '88 Notre Dame	8009BF120087
Home Team as '73 Notre Dame	8009BF120086
Home Team as '94 Nebraska	8009BF120085
Home Team as '93 Nebraska	8009BF120084
Home Team as '91 Nebraska	8009BF120083
Home Team as '83 Nebraska	8009BF120082
Home Team as '91 Michigan	8009BF120081
Home Team as '65 Michigan State	8009BF120080
Home Team as '94 Miami	8009BF12007F
Home Team as '92 Miami	8009BF12007E
Home Team as '91 Miami	8009BF12007D
Home Team as '89 Miami	8009BF12007C
Home Team as '87 Miami	8009BF12007B
Home Team as '86 Miami	8009BF12007A
Home Team as '83 Miami	8009BF120079
Home Team as '82 Georgia	8009BF120078
Home Team as '96 Florida State	8009BF120077
Home Team as '93 Florida State	8009BF120076
Home Team as '96 Florida	8009BF120075
Home Team as '89 Colorado	8009BF120074
Home Team as '92 Alabama	8009BF120073
Home Team as '89 Alabama	8009BF120072
Home Team as '78 Alabama	8009BF120071
Home Team as '73 Alabama	8009BF120070
All Extra Teams and Stadiums	8009B790FFFF
All Extra Teams and Stadiums	8009B792FFFF
All Extra Teams and Stadiums	8009B79403FF

NCAA GAMEBREAKER '98
Away Team Scores 0 . . . . 8010206C0000
Home Team Scores 0 801020680000
Away Team Scores 99 . . . . 8010206C0063
Home Team Scores 99 801020680063

NEED FOR SPEED II
Engine Upgrade 80035B800001
Extra Car and Track 800E292A0803

NEED FOR SPEED V-RALLY
Infinite Credits 800BACA40009

NFL GAMEDAY '97
Away Team Scores 0 . . . . 800CA0500000
Home Team Scores 0 . . . . 800CA04C0000

NFL QUARTERBACK CLUB '97
Away Team Scores 0 . . . . 800D3ACA0000
Home Team Scores 0 . . . . 800D14C60000

NHL FACEOFF
Other Team Scores 0 . . . . 800E780C0000

NHL FACEOFF '97
Away Team Scores 0 . . . . 800DD9560000
Away Team Scores 0 . . . . 800EB1A40000
Home Team Scores 0 . . . . 800DDB7C0000
Home Team Scores 0 . . . . 800EB1A20000

NHL OPEN ICE
Away Team Scores 0 . . . . 8005E7060000
Home Team Scores 0 . . . . 8005E6FE0000

NHL POWERPLAY
Away Team Scores 0 . . . . 800114B40000
Away Team Scores 0 . . . . 801EABB40000
Away Team Scores 0 . . . . 801E22BC0000

NHL POWERPLAY '98

Away Team: Rad Army All-Stars	30010293002D
Away Team: Virgin Blasters	30010293002C
Home Team: Rad Army All-Stars	30010292002D
Home Team: Virgin Blasters	30010292002C

NIGHTMARE CREATURES

Berzerker	800CC06A0009
Chaos	800CC0700009
Dynamite	800CC0620009
Fire Bombs	800CC0660009
Flash	800CC0640009
Freeze	800CC0600009
Healing	800CC06E0009
Infinite Credits	800CC0060009
Multi-Gun	800CC0680009
Pistol	800CC0720009
Proximity Mines	800CC05C0009
Repulsive Smoke	800CC05E0009
Super Healing	800CC06C0009

NORSE BY NORSEWEST

Infinite Health Character 1	800B92040003
Infinite Health Character 2	800B92200003
Infinite Health Character 3	800B923C0003

NUCLEAR STRIKE

Infinite Ammo	8005A9380000
Infinite Ammo	8005A93A0000
Infinite Fuel	800399980000
Infinite Fuel	8003999A0000

OFF WORLD INTERCEPTOR

Infinite Money	800CD878C350
Infinite Money	800CD87A9700

OLYMPIC SOCCER
Team 1 Never Scores (Arcade) .... .801A7D8C0000
Team 2 Never Scores (Arcade) .... .801B0BA40000

ONE
Infinite Lives 8010BA8C0005
Infinite Ammo. 8010AC3CFFFF
Infinite Ammo. 8010B6D8FFFF

OVERBLOOD
Allen Wrench .800EF5380001
Anti-Gravity Device 800EF4F00001
Broken Thermostat 800EF4FC0001
Burner 800EF5200001
Capsule 800EF5040001
Charged Battery 800EF5480001
Chemicals Bottle 800EF5000001
Compact Data Disc 800EF52C0001
Dead Battery 800EF5440001
Emergency Spray 800EF5340001
Hand Gun 800EF5080001
Identification Card 800EF54C0001
Infinite Health 800CF8F40064
Iron Rods 800EF5140001
Laser Knife .800EF4EC0001
Memo 800EF4E80001
Memory Chip 800EF4E00001
Metal Grate 800EF51C0001
Oil Container 800EF4F80001
Red Card 800EF5280001
Sample Case 800EF4F40001
Silver Key .800EF50C0001
Stun Gun 800EF5180001

PANDEMONIUM 2
Coins 800ABD7801F8
Infinite Health. 800ABD760010
Infinite Lives 800ABD740010

PANZER GENERAL
Infinite Prestige 800EDB8407D0

PARAPPA THE RAPPER
Always Rap Cool 801C368E0000
Always Score 999 Points. 801C367003E7

PEAK PERFORMANCE
Place 1st 8009CA0C0000
Place 1st 800A1FF2000

PERFECT WEAPON
Infinite Health 8011ADAC0BD6

PHILOSOMA
Infinite Buster Grenades 800E7F5C0003
Infinite Credits 800E7D280003
Infinite Lives 800E7CA40002
Infinite Shields 800E7F600004
Maximum A-Break .800E7D100002
Maximum Laser 800E7D0E0002
Maximum RAV-B 800E7D120002
Maximum Vulcan Cannon 800E7D0C0002
SRM Missiles 800E80040002

PGA TOUR '98
Only One Shot Recorded. 800906C80001
Only One Shot Recorded. 800907AC0001
Only One Shot Recorded. 800BAE380100

PITBALL
Team 1 Scores 0 . . . . .800980CC0000
Team 2 Scores 0 . . . . .800980D00000

PO'ED
Have BFD And Flame Thrower 8009ABBC0101
Have Drill 8009ABBA0101
Have Jetpack 8009ABA80032
Have Jetpack 8009AC700100
Have Knife 8009ABB80101
Have Missile Cam .8009ABC20001
Have Pulsegun And Meatseeker 8009ABC00101
Have Wailer And Rocket Launch 8009ABBE0101
Infinite Ammo For Pulse/BFD 8009ABA403E7
Infinite Flamer Ammo 8009ABA803E7
Infinite Health 80075C400064
Infinite Health 8009ABA00064
Infinite Meatseeker Meat 8009ABB003E7
Infinite Rockets 8009ABB403E7
Infinite Wailer Ammo 8009ABAC03E7

PORSCHE CHALLENGE
Hyper Car and Invisible Car 800CA5BE0101

POWERSLAVE
All Artifacts	80084C00FFFF
All Keys	80084C02FFFF
Amun Bombs	80084BE2003C
Cobra Staff	80084BE6003C
Infinite Health	80084BBA00C8
Manacles	80084BEA003C
Map	80084C0CFFFF
Ring of Ra	80084BE8003C
Transmitter	80084C06FFFF

POY POY
Infinite Health P1	800DCB6800C8
Infinite Health P1	800DCB6A00C8

PRIMAL RAGE
Infinite Health P1	8009A8040000
Infinite Health P1	800A7DEA0000
Infinite Health P2	8009A80C0000
Infinite Health P2	800A7E7E0000
Infinite Time	8009A1EC0064

PRO-PINBALL
Infinite Balls	800631D80001
Maximum Bonus	80063308000A

PROJECT OVERKILL
Digiprint Hand	8005BDA40001
Have Green Key	8005BD9E0001
Have Orange Key	8005BDA20001
Have Yellow Key	8005BDA00001
Infinite Ammo P1	800997DA0064
Infinite Ammo P1	800997DC6464
Infinite Ammo P1	800997DE0064
Infinite Health P1	800997B60164
Scanner Eye	8005BD9C0101

PROJECT: HORNED OWL
Infinite Grenades 800B94C60518
Infinite Grenades P2 .800B94D60518
Infinite Health 800B94BE0064
Infinite Health P2 . . . . .800B94CE0064

PSYCHIC FORCE
Infinite Health PI 80101E5403E8
Infinite Health P2 . . . . .80101F9803E8
Infinite Psychic Power PI 80101E560190
Infinite Psychic Power P2 . . . . .80101F9A0190
No Psychic Power PI .80101E560000
No Psychic Power P2 .80101F9A0000

RAGE RACER
Darwin Awards' JATO Car 8009E4800AAF
Extra Cash 8019C610FFFF
Infinite Cash 8019C610C9FF
Infinite Cash 8019C6123B9A
Infinite Race Tries 801E3FFA0005
Place 1st 8009E53C0001

RAIDEN PROJECT
Infinite Credits 8004D5DA0003
Infinite Lives PI 8012F7F40003
Infinite Lives P2 . . . . .8012F8240003
Infinite Thermo-Nukes PI 8012F8020003
Infinite Thermo-Nukes P2 . . . . .8012F8320003
Maximum Homing Missiles PI 8012F8000004
Maximum Homing Missiles P2 . . . . .8012F8300004
Maximum Lasers PI .8012F7FC0008
Maximum Lasers P2 .8012F82C0008
Maximum Nuke Missiles PI 8012F7FE0004
Maximum Nuke Missiles P2 . . . . .8012F82E0004
Maximum Vulcan PI .8012F7FA0008
Maximum Vulcan P2 .8012F82A0008

RAIDEN PROJECT II
Infinite Credits 800FFC240003
Infinite Lives P1 . . . . .800ECF400003
Infinite Lives P2 . . . . .800ECF800003
Maximum Homing Missiles P1 . . . . .800ECF320004
Maximum Homing Missiles P2 . . . . .800ECF720004
Maximum Lasers P1 . . . . .800EFC2A0008
Maximum Lasers P2 . . . . .800ECF6A0008
Maximum Nuke Missiles P1 . . . . .800ECF300004
Maximum Nuke Missiles P2 . . . . .800ECF700004
Maximum Plasma P1 . . . . .800ECF2C0008
Maximum Plasma P2 . . . . .800ECF6C0008
Maximum Vulcan P1 . . . . .800ECF280008
Maximum Vulcan P2 . . . . .800ECF680008

RALLY CROSS
Extra Cars 800552780014
Extra Tracks And Cars 800564560114

RAMPAGE WORLD TOUR
Infinite Health George 800D67860063
Infinite Health Lizzy 800D69520063
Infinite Health Ralph. 800D6B1E0063

RAYMAN
Infinite Health 801F62000002
Infinite Lives 801E4D500060
Master Code D000853440A0
Mega Glove Power .800AE9C80D0D

REBEL ASSAULT II
Infinite Armor 800C07CC1000

RELOADED
Infinite Ammo P1+2 . . . . .80081D9C0000
Infinite Bombs P1+2 800817800000
Infinite Lives P1+2 .800815000000
Infinite Lives P1+2 .800815020000

RESIDENT EVIL

Bazooka in 1st Pos.	800C8784FF07
Colt Python 127 rounds	800C8784FF04
Flame Thrower in 1st Pos.	800C8784FF06
Infinite Health	800C51AC0060
Rocket Launcher In 1st Pos.	800C8784FF0A
Shotgun in 1st Pos.	800c8784ff03
Start w/Acid Bazooka in Chest.	D00C867C0010
Start w/Acid Bazooka in Chest.	800C8778FF08
Start w/Baretta in Chest.	D00C867C0010
Start w/Baretta in Chest.	800C8772FF02
Start w/Bazooka in Chest.	D00C867C0010
Start w/Bazooka in Chest.	800C877AFF07
Start w/Colt in Chest.	D00C867C0010
Start w/Colt in Chest.	800C877EFF05
Start w/Flame Bazooka in Chest.	D00C867C0010
Start w/Flame Bazooka in Chest.	800C8776FF09
Start w/Flame Thrower in Chest.	D00C867C0010
Start w/Flame Thrower in Chest.	800C877CFF06
Start w/Rocket Launcher in Chest	D00C867C0010
Start w/Rocket Launcher in Chest	800C8774FF0A
Start w/Shotgun in Chest	D00C867C0010
Start w/Shotgun in Chest	800C8782FF03
Triangle Button Restores Health.	D00CF8440010
Triangle Button Restores Health.	800C51AC00C8
L2 + Triangle Button for Shotgun	D00CF8441001
L2 + Triangle Button for Shotgun	800C8784FF03
L2 + Circle Button for Barretta	D00CF8442001
L2 + Circle Button for Barretta	800C8784FF04
L2 + X Button for Colt Python	D00CF8444001
L2 + X Button for Colt Python	800C8784FF05
L2 + Square Button for Flame Thrower	D00CF8448001
L2 + Square Button for Flame Thrower	800C8784FF06
L1 + Triangle Button for Bazooka	D00CF8441004
L1 + Triangle Button for Bazooka	800C8784FF07
L1 + Circle Button for Acid Bazooka	D00CF8442004
L1 + Circle Button for Acid Bazooka	800C8784FF08
L1 + X Button for Flame Bazooka	D00CF8444004
L1 + X Button for Flame Bazooka	800C8784FF09
L1 + Square Button for Rocket Launcher	D00CF8448004
L1 + Square Button for Rocket Launcher	800C8784FF0A

RESIDENT EVIL 2
Playing as Leon

Infinite Health	800C7E7A00C8
Anti-Venom	800C7F3C0000
L1+L2 Health Restore	D00C646C0005
L1+L2 Health Restore	800C7E7A00C8
Start w/ Custom Handgun in Crate	D00AAC8C1000
Start w/ Custom Handgun in Crate	800CCB94FF04
Start w/ Magnum in Crate	D00AAC8C1000
Start w/ Magnum in Crate	800CCB98FF05
Start w/ Custom Magnum in Crate	D00AAC8C1000
Start w/ Custom Magnum in Crate	800CCB9CFF06
Start w/ Shotgun in Crate	D00AAC8C1000
Start w/ Shotgun in Crate	800CCBA0FF07
Start w/ Custom Shotgun in Crate	D00AAC8C1000
Start w/ Custom Shotgun in Crate	800CCBA4FF08
Start w/ Colt S.A.A. in Crate	D00AAC8C1000
Start w/ Colt S.A.A. in Crate	800CCBA8FF0D
Start w/ Submachine Gun in Crate	D00AAC8C1000
Start w/ Submachine Gun in Crate	800CCBACFF0F
Start w/ Flamethrower in Crate	D00AAC8C1000
Start w/ Flamethrower in Crate	800CCBB0FF10
Start w/ Rocket Launcher in Crate	D00AAC8C1000
Start w/ Rocket Launcher in Crate	800CCBB4FF11
Start w/ Gatling Gun in Crate	D00AAC8C1000
Start w/ Gatling Gun in Crate	800CCBB8FF12
Start w/ ink Ribbons in Crate	D00AAC8C1000
Start w/ ink Ribbons in Crate	800CCC90FF1E
Start w/ Small Key in Crate	D00AAC8C1000
Start w/ Small Key in Crate	800CCC8C031F
Start w/ Red Jewel in Crate	D00AAC8C1000
Start w/ Red Jewel in Crate	800CCC880133
Start w/ Cord in Crate	D00AAC8C1000
Start w/ Cord in Crate	800CCC800156
Start w/ Fuse Case in Crate	D00AAC8C1000
Start w/ Fuse Case in Crate	800CCC7C014D
Start w/ Bishop Plug in Crate	D00AAC8C1000
Start w/ Bishop Plug in Crate	800CCC78013B
Start w/ Rook Plug in Crate	D00AAC8C1000
Start w/ Rook Plug in Crate	800CCC74013C
Start w/ Knight Plug in Crate	D00AAC8C1000
Start w/ Knight Plug in Crate	800CCC70013D
Start w/ King Plug in Crate	D00AAC8C1000
Start w/ King Plug in Crate	800CCC6C013E
Start w/ Unicorn Medal in Crate	D00AAC8C1000
Start w/ Unicorn Medal in Crate	800CCC640147
Start w/ Eagle Medal in Crate	D00AAC8C1000
Start w/ Eagle Medal in Crate	800CCC600148
Start w/ Wolf Medal in Crate	D00AAC8C1000
Start w/ Wolf Medal in Crate	800CCC5C0149

Start w/ G-Virus in Crate	**D00AAC8C1000**
Start w/ G-Virus in Crate	**800CCC580152**
Start w/ Special Key in Crate	**D00AAC8C1000**
Start w/ Special Key in Crate	**800CCC540153**
Start w/ Cabin Key in Crate	**D00AAC8C1000**
Start w/ Cabin Key in Crate	**800CCC500158**
Start w/ Precinct Key in Crate	**D00AAC8C1000**
Start w/ Precinct Key in Crate	**800CCC4C0159**
Start w/ Lockpick in Crate	**D00AAC8C1000**
Start w/ Lockpick in Crate	**800CCC480130**
Start w/ Lab Card Key in Crate	**D00AAC8C1000**
Start w/ Lab Card Key in Crate	**800CCC440161**
Start w/ Master Key in Crate	**D00AAC8C1000**
Start w/ Master Key in Crate	**800CCC400162**
Start w/ Platform Key in Crate	**D00AAC8C1000**
Start w/ Platform Key in Crate	**800CCC3C0163**
L1+Triangle for Magnum	**D00C646C0014**
L1+Triangle for Magnum	**800CCB68FF05**
L1+X for Custom Magnum	**D00C646C0044**
L1+X for Custom Magnum	**800CCB68FF06**
L1+Square for Shotgun	**D00C646C0084**
L1+Square for Shotgun	**800CCB68FF07**
L2+Triangle for Custom Shotgun	**D00C646C0011**
L2+Triangle for Custom Shotgun	**800CCB68FF08**
L2+X for Colt S.A.A.	**D00C646C0041**
L2+X for Colt S.A.A.	**800CCB68FF0D**
L2+Square for Sumachine Gun	**D00C646C0081**
L2+Square for Sumachine Gun	**800CCB68FF0F**
R2+Triangle for Flamethrower	**D00C646C0012**
R2+Triangle for Flamethrower	**800CCB68FF10**
R2+X for Rocket Launcher	**D00C646C0042**
R2+X for Rocket Launcher	**800CCB68FF11**
R2+Square for Gatling Gun	**D00C646C0082**
R2+Square for Gatling Gun	**800CCB68FF12**
Rocket Launcher in 1st Pos.	**800CCB68FF11**

Playing as Claire

Start w/ Ink Ribbons in Crate	**D013A2B20250**
Start w/ Ink Ribbons in Crate	**800CCA58FF1E**
Start w/ Small Key in Crate	**D013A2B20250**
Start w/ Small Key in Crate	**800CCA54031F**
Start w/ Red Jewel in Crate	**D013A2B20250**
Start w/ Red Jewel in Crate	**800CCA500133**
Start w/ Cord in Crate	**D013A2B20250**
Start w/ Cord in Crate	**800CCA4C0156**
Start w/ Fuse Case in Crate	**D013A2B20250**
Start w/ Fuse Case in Crate	**800CCA48014D**
Start w/ Bishop Plug in Crate	**D013A2B20250**
Start w/ Bishop Plug in Crate	**800CCA44013B**
Start w/ Rook Plug in Crate	**D013A2B20250**
Start w/ Rook Plug in Crate	**800CCA40013C**
Start w/ Knight Plug in Crate	**D013A2B20250**

Start w/ Knight Plug in Crate	800CCA3C013D
Start w/ King Plug in Crate.	D013A2B20250
Start w/ King Plug in Crate.	800CCA38013E
Start w/ Unicorn Medal in Crate	D013A2B20250
Start w/ Unicorn Medal in Crate	800CCA340147
Start w/ Eagle Medal in Crate	D013A2B20250
Start w/ Eagle Medal in Crate	800CCA300148
Start w/ Wolf Medal in Crate	D013A2B20250
Start w/ Wolf Medal in Crate	800CCA2C0149
Start w/ G-Virus in Crate.	D013A2B20250
Start w/ G-Virus in Crate.	800CCA280152
Start w/ Special Key in Crate	D013A2B20250
Start w/ Special Key in Crate	800CCA240153
Start w/ Cabin Key in Crate	D013A2B20250
Start w/ Cabin Key in Crate	800CCA200158
Start w/ Precinct Key in Crate	D013A2B20250
Start w/ Precinct Key in Crate	800CCA1C0159
Start w/ Lockpick in Crate	D013A2B20250
Start w/ Lockpick in Crate	800CCA180130
Start w/ Lab Card Key in Crate	D013A2B20250
Start w/ Lab Card Key in Crate	800CCA140161
Start w/ Master Key in Crate	D013A2B20250
Start w/ Master Key in Crate	800CCA100162
Start w/ Platform Key in Crate	D013A2B20250
Start w/ Platform Key in Crate	800CCA0C0163
Start w/ Grenade Launcher in Crate.	D013A2B20250
Start w/ Grenade Launcher in Crate.	800CC95CFF09
Start w/ Grenade Launcher (Fire) in Crate. . .	D013A2B20250
Start w/ Grenade Launcher (Fire) in Crate. . .	800CC960FF0A
Start w/ Grenade Launcher (Acid) in Crate . .	D013A2B20250
Start w/ Grenade Launcher (Acid) in Crate . .	800CC964FF0B
Start w/ Bowgun in Crate.	D013A2B20250
Start w/ Bowgun in Crate.	800CC968FF0C
Start w/ Colt S.A.A. in Crate	D013A2B20250
Start w/ Colt S.A.A. in Crate	800CC96CFF0D
Start w/ Spark Shot in Crate	D013A2B20250
Start w/ Spark Shot in Crate	800CC970FF0E
Start w/ Submachine Gun in Crate.	D013A2B20250
Start w/ Submachine Gun in Crate.	800CC974FF0F
Start w/ Rocket Launcher in Crate.	D013A2B20250
Start w/ Rocket Launcher in Crate.	800CC978FF11
Start w/ Gatling Gun in Crate.	D013A2B20250
Start w/ Gatling Gun in Crate.	800CC97CFF12
Infinite Health.	800C7C4200C8
L1+L2 Health Restore	D00C623C0005
L1+L2 Health Restore	800C7C4200C8
L1+Triangle for Grenade Launcher	D00C623C0014
L1+Triangle for Grenade Launcher	800CC930FF09
L1+X for Grenade Launcher (Fire).	D00C623C0044
L1+X for Grenade Launcher (Fire).	800CC930FF0A

L1+Square for Grenade Launcher (Acid)	**D00C623C0084**
L1+Square for Grenade Launcher (Acid)	**800CC930FF0B**
L2+Triangle for Bowgun	**D00C623C0011**
L2+Triangle for Bowgun	**800CC930FF0C**
L2+X for Colt S.A.A.	**D00C623C0041**
L2+X for Colt S.A.A.	**800CC930FF0D**
L2+Square for Spark Shot.	**D00C623C0081**
L2+Square for Spark Shot.	**800CC930FF0E**
R2+Triangle for Submachine Gun	**D00C623C0012**
R2+Triangle for Submachine Gun	**800CC930FF0F**
R2+X for Rocket Launcher.	**D00C623C0042**
R2+X for Rocket Launcher.	**800CC930FF11**
R2+Square for Gatling Gun	**D00C623C0082**
R2+Square for Gatling Gun	**800CC930FF12**

NOTE: Don't equip any weapons to the secondary characters in this game. This will cause the game to lock up and may cause loss of Game Save information. Codes for Leon are designed specifically for Leon and are not to be used with Ada. Codes for Claire are specifically designed for Claire and are not for use with Sherry. If these items show up within the secondary character's menu, do not equip them. The game will not lock up if they are in the menu, but will lock up if they are equipped.

RETURN FIRE

Infinite Ammo	.800820300096
Infinite Ammo	.800820400032
Infinite Armor	.800820220004
Infinite Fuel	.800820160180

RIDGE RACER

Use Black Car	.80080196000C

RIDGE RACER REVOLUTION

Course Select	.801DC9C80707
Extra Cars	.801DD2080001
Race as Black Car	.8007C43A000C
Race as Black Kid Car	.8007C43A000D
Race as White Car	.8007C43A000E

RISE 2 RESURRECTION

Infinite Health P1 ....8007D3C60078
Infinite Health P2 ....8007D4620078
Infinite Time 800672EC0000
No Health P2 ....8007D4620000

ROAD RASH

Infinite Cash 800DAD40FFFF

ROBO PIT

Infinite Energy P1 ....800A7E0C0096
Infinite Energy P2 ....800A7E0E0096

ROBOTRON X

Infinite Lives P1 ....800264A40000
Infinite Lives P1 ....800264A60000

RUSH HOUR

Extra Vehicles 801074D4FFFF
Infinite Time 801042BC0064
Reverse Mode 801074D6FFFF
Super Championship Mode 801074D8FFFF

SAMURAI SHODOWN III

Infinite Health P1 ....800185B40080
Infinite Health P2 ....800186B40080
No Health P1 ....800185B40000
No Health P2 ....800186B40000

SHELLSHOCK

Air Support 800855B40004
Armor Upgrade 800855AC0032
Coolant 800855BE0004
Engine Upgrade 800855B60004
Infinite Armor 80087C1E0300
Infinite Cash 800855C0FFFF
Reloader 800855BA0004
SAMS Rockets 800855AE0004
Target Computer 800855BC0004
Track Upgrade 800855B80004

SHIPWRECKERS!
Infinite Ammo 800B862C0000

SHOCKWAVE ASSAULT
Infinite Lasers 8006EBDC2C2B

SIM CITY 2000
Infinite Cash 800EA8B0FFFF

SKELETON WARRIORS
Infinite Health 801DB7600064
Infinite Lives 801DB7680064
Infinite Starsword 801DB7740064

SLAM 'N' JAM
Away Team Scores 0 . . . . 800EB7040000
Home Team Scores 0 . . . . 800EB5200000

SLAMSCAPE
Infinite Armor 801842A80200
Infinite Armor 801842B00200
Infinite Fastblasters 800F6C0A0064
Infinite Fastblasters 801842C00280
Infinite Mines 801842C80064
Infinite Ripstars 801842C40064
Infinite Torps 801842CC0064

SOUL BLADE
All Weapons for Sophitia 800EA34AFFFF
All Weapons for Sophitia 800EA360FFFF
All Weapons for Cervantes 800EA352FFFF
All Weapons for Cervantes 800EA368FFFF
All Weapons for Hwang 800EA350FFFF
All Weapons for Hwang 800EA366FFFF
All Weapons for Li Long 800EA346FFFF
All Weapons for Li Long 800EA35CFFFF
All Weapons for Mitsurugi 800EA340FFFF
All Weapons for Mitsurugi 800EA356FFFF
All Weapons for Rock 800EA34EFFFF
All Weapons for Rock 800EA364FFFF
All Weapons for Seigfried 800EA34CFFFF
All Weapons for Seigfried 800EA362FFFF

GameShark Pocket Power Guide

All Weapons for Seung	.800EA342FFFF
All Weapons for Seung	.800EA358FFFF
All Weapons for Taki	.800EA344FFFF
All Weapons for Taki	.800EA35AFFFF
All Weapons for Voldo	.800EA348FFFF
All Weapons for Voldo	.800EA35EFFFF
Infinite Health P1	.800BFFBA00F0
Infinite Health P2	.800C2EF200F0
Infinite Power Moves P1	.800C01160060
Infinite Power Moves P2	.800C304E0060
Low Health P1	.800BFFBA0000
Low Health P2	.800C2EF20000
No Power Moves P1	.800C01160000
No Power Moves P2	.800C304E0000

SOVIET STRIKE

Infinite Ammo	.8004C1F00000
Infinite Ammo	.8004C1F20000
Infinite Armor	.80075D6805DC
Infinite Armor	.8008368005DC
Infinite Fuel	.8002D83C0000
Infinite Fuel	.8002D83E0000

SPACE GRIFFON

Infinite Energy	.801E00581F40
Infinite Rocket Launcher	.801E00320190
Infinite Rocket Launcher	.801E0036000C

SPAWN

Infinite Health	8007F0500860
Low Enemy Health	8007F1600000
R1 Power Drain	D007F1440008
R1 Power Drain	8007F1600000

SPIDER—THE VIDEO GAME
Infinite Health 8001642A0002

STAR FIGHTER
Infinite Armor 801051DC0080

Infinite ATA Missiles .80166B80000A
Infinite ATG Missiles .80166B7C000A
Infinite Beam Lasers 80166B8803E7
Infinite Lives 80062ADC0009
Infinite Mega-Bombs 80166B8403E7
Infinite Mines 80166B9003E7
Infinite Multi-Missiles 80166B8C0009

STAR GLADIATOR
Extra Characters 801EA8E40101
Extra Characters 801EA8E60001
Infinite Health PI 801D7A0400C8
Infinite Health PI 801D7CA000C8
Infinite Health P2 . . . . .801D7A0600C8
Infinite Health P2 . . . . .801D821800C8
Longsword Hayato 801CC5F81500
Longsword Hayato 801CC6001C00
Longsword Hayato 801CC6DC1500
Longsword Hayato 801CC6E01C00
Longsword Hayato 801D7E1401C0
Longsword Hayato 801D7E1601C0

STAR WARS: MASTERS OF TERÄS KÄSI
Infinite Health PI 800AC2741000
Infinite Health P2 . . . . 800AC28C1000
Low Health PI 800AC2740000
Low Health P2 . . . . 800AC28C0000
Extra Characters 800BEF5EFFFF
Full Power PI 800AC278FFFF
Full Power P2 . . . . 800AC290FFFF
No Power PI 800AC2780000
No Power P2 . . . . 800AC2900000
Press Select for Jedi Mind Trick PI D00802C40100
Press Select for Jedi Mind Trick PI 800AC28C0000

STEEL REIGN
Infinite Cannon 800B77080008
Infinite Guided Missiles 800B76AE0008
Infinite Ion Cannon 800B76780100

Infinite Laser I	800B76540100
Infinite Laser II	800B76660100
Infinite Mines	800B76F60010
Infinite Phoenix Missiles	800B76C00008
Infinite Plasma	800B768A0100
Extra Shields	800B75640100
Infinite Specials	800B76D200E8

STREET FIGHTER—THE MOVIE

Infinite Health P1	801B759A0070
Infinite Health P2	801B793C0070

STREET FIGHTER ALPHA

Infinite Health P1	8018710C0090
Infinite Health P2	801873D40090

STREET FIGHTER ALPHA 2

Infinite Health P1	801981F20090
Infinite Health P1	801981F00090
Infinite Health P2	801985840090
Infinite Health P2	801985860090

STREET FIGHTER EX PLUS A

Infinite Health P1	801D63B4C8C8
Low Health P1	801D63B40000

STRIKE POINT

Infinite Armor P1	8011CFDC1900
Infinite ATG And ATA Missiles	8011D0BA6363
Infinite Bombs And Turbos	8011D0BC6363
Infinite Lives	8011D0F60004

SUB-ZERO MK MYTHOLOGIES

Infinite Lives	800D7D480002

SUIKODEN

Infinite HP Cleo	801B838803E7
Infinite HP Cleo	801B838A03E7

Infinite HP Gremio 801B82E803E7
Infinite HP Gremio 801B82EA03E7
Infinite HP PI 801B829803E7
Infinite HP PI 801B829A03E7
Infinite HP Pahn 801B833803E7
Infinite HP Pahn 801B833A03E7
Infinite HP Ted 801B83D803E7
Infinite HP Ted 801B83DA03E7
Quick Level Gain Cleo 801B8392FFFF
Quick Level Gain Gremio 801B82F2FFFF
Quick Level Gain Pahn 801B8342FFFF
Quick Level Gain Ted 801B83E2FFFF
Super Power Cleo 301B83940063
Super Power Gremio 301B82F40063
Super Power Pahn 301B83440063
Super Power Ted 301B83E40063

SWAGMAN
Infinite Health Zack 801090080005

TAIL OF THE SUN
Complete Tower 800CA0A000FF
Have Spear 800C55280009
Have Spear 800CA08C0009

TECMO SUPERBOWL
Away Team Scores 0 ....8005CE7A0000
Home Team Scores 0 ....8005CE760000
Infinite Gold 800A3868FFFF
Infinite Health 800A37E26464
Infinite MP 800A3860FFFF

TECMO'S DECEPTION
Infinite Gold 800A3868FFFF
Infinite Health 800A37E26464
Infinite MP 800A3860FFFF

TEKKEN
Infinite Health PI 801232DE0080
Infinite Health P2 801243120080
No Health P2 801243120000
Select All Extra Players 801273D0FFFF
Select All Extra Players 801273D200FF

TEKKEN 2

Extra Characters	.801ED1D41A20
Extra Characters	.801ED1D6142A
Extra Characters	.801ED1D81E22
Extra Characters	.801ED1DA1816
Extra Characters	.801ED1DC281C
Extra Characters	.801ED1E80016
Infinite Health PI	.800D09EA006E
Infinite Health P2	.800D1BF2006E

TEMPEST X

Infinite Lives	.8009931A0009

TENKA

Blue Key	.800519CC0001
Burst Laser	.80019DEA0001
Double Shot	.80019DE20001
Dual Laser	.80019DE80001
Green Key	.800519CA0001
Grenade	.80019DEE0001
Infinite Ammo	.80059A6C0063
Infinite Ammo	.80059A780063
Infinite Armor	.80019DDA00C8
Infinite Health	.80019DD80064
Infinite Laser Power	.80059A700014
Infinite Missiles	.8003B5C40004
Infinite Missiles	.80059A7A0004
Missile	.80019DEC0001
Purple Key	.800519D00001
Rapid Fire	.80019DE40001
Red Key	.800519C80001
Single Laser	.80019DE60001
Yellow Key	.800519CE0001

TEST DRIVE 4

999 Points	.8007F1C203E7

TEST DRIVE OFF ROAD
4X4 Buggy	800B4A8C0001
Extra Tracks	800B1978000C
Hotrod and Monster Truck	800B4A8A0101
Stockcar	800B4A880001

TETRIS PLUS
Ceiling Never Drops	800455B6000A
Ceiling Never Drops	80045D76FFFA
Ceiling Never Drops	800EE39C0000
Ceiling Never Drops	800EE916000A
No Timer	800EE5800001
Pause	800F2CEC000F
Pause	800F35C0660E

THEME PARK
Infinite Money	801AF850FFFF

THUNDER TRUCK RALLY
0 Car Crush Points P2	800BB0C20000
Extra Car Crush Points P1	800BB0C003E7
Infinite Armor	801DBE100000

THUNDERSTRIKE II
Infinite Ammo	80074E7A008E
Infinite Ammo	80074E7C002E
Infinite Ammo	80074E7E002E
Infinite Armor	80074D04008E

TIGERSHARK
Infinite Armor	800BFEF400F0
Infinite Armor	800BFEF600F0
Infinite ECM-9000's	800BFF500013
Infinite ECM Torpedoes	800BFF520013
Infinite EMP Torpedoes	800BFF440013
Infinite Gatling Ammo	800BFF3801FF
Infinite Lives	800847980003

Infinite MK-60's 800BFF3C0013
Infinite MK-65's 800BFF3E0013
Infinite MK-77's 800BFF420013
Infinite MK-90's 800BFF460013
Infinite SM-19's 800BFF480013
Infinite SM-25's 800BFF4A0013
Infinite SR-70's 800BFF4C0013
Laser Never Overheats 800BFF3A07D0

TIME COMMANDO
Infinite Health 800979820020
Infinite Lives 800979A00302

TIME CRISIS
Infinite Health. 800B20C00005
Infinite Time 800B1D641000
Low Course Time 800B1DBC0010
Low Course Time. 800B1DF80010
Infinite Credits 800B1D5C0009
Auto-Reload. 800B1DDC0006

TOKYO HIGHWAY BATTLE
Infinite Funds 8006debcffff
Triangle Button Turbo Boost. D006E2C00010
Triangle Button Turbo Boost. 800C3FEA000F

TOMB RAIDER
Infinite Air 801DDF020708
Infinite Magnum Ammo 801DDF940032
Infinite Uzi Ammo 801DDFA00032

TOMB RAIDER VERSION 1.1
Have All Guns 8008872C0005
Have All Items 8008872C0008
Infinite Air 801DE0020708
Infinite Magnum Ammo 801DE09403E7
Infinite Shotgun Shells 801DE0AC03E7
Infinite Uzi Ammo 801DE0A003E7

TOMB RAIDER 2

Infinite Air	8008C4FE0708
All Items	80088AA0000B
All Items	80088ADC80C8
All Items	80088AE08020
All Items	80088AE48218
All Items	80088AE8850C
All Items	80088AEC8560
All Items	80088AF0811C
All Items	80088AF48074
All Items	80088AF88170
All Items	80088AFC826C
All Items	80088B0081C4
Infinite M16 Ammo	8008C5C003E8
Infinite Auto Pistol Ammo	8008C5AC03E8
Infinite Shotgun Shells	8008C5B403E8
Infinite Uzi Ammo	8008C5B003E8
Infinite Grenades	8008C5BC03E8
Infinite Harpoons	8008C5B803E8
Infinite Flares	80088AAE000A

TOP GUN

Infinite AGM Missiles	801CFECC0064
Infinite MIRV Missiles	801CFEC00064
Infinite Standard Missiles	801CFECA0064
Infinite Surefires	801CFEBC0064
Infinite U238's	801CFEBE0064

TOTAL ECLIPSE TURBO

Infinite Lives	800766A00005
Infinite Plasma Bombs	80078DD40003
Infinite Shield	80079048FB50

TREASURES OF THE DEEP

Infinite Cash	800406C20FFF

TRIPLE PLAY '98

Away Team Scores 0	300269C80000
Away Team Scores 25	300269C80019
Extra Stadiums	80102EEC0001
Home Team Scores 0	300269C40000
Home Team Scores 25	300269C40019
Play as EA Dream Team	80021E7C0100

TRUE PINBALL

Infinite Balls	800441D40001

TUNNEL B1

Infinite Time	800C40B60031

TWISTED METAL

Infinite Armor	801A19140080
Infinite Catapults	801A1C0C0002
Infinite Fire Missiles	801A1C000002
Infinite Freeze Missiles	801A1C020002
Infinite Homing Missiles	801A1C040002
Infinite Mines	801A1C100002
Infinite Oil	801A1C120002
Infinite Power Missiles	801A1C060002
Infinite Rear Flame	801A1C0E0002
Infinite Rear Missiles	801A1C0A0002
Infinite Specials	801A1C160014
Infinite Tag Missiles	801A1C080002
Infinite Tire Spikes	801A1C140002

TWISTED METAL 2

Advanced Attacks	801883080400
Advanced Attacks P2	80188B1C0400
All Infinite Weapons P1	801882DA0F0F
All Infinite Weapons P2	80188AEE0F0F
Extra Vehicles	80180D040101
Infinite Armor	80187D000096
Infinite Armor P2	801885140096
Infinite Fire Missiles	801882EE0009
Infinite Fire Missiles P2	80188AFC0009
Infinite Homing Missiles	801882EA0009
Infinite Homing Missiles P2	80188AFE0009
Infinite Lightning	801882F40009
Infinite Lightning P2	80188B080009
Infinite Napalm	801882F00009
Infinite Napalm P2	80188B040009

Infinite Power Missiles **801882E80009**
Infinite Power Missiles P2 ....**80188B020009**
Infinite Remote Bombs **801882EC0009**
Infinite Remote Bombs P2 ....**80188B000009**
Infinite Ricochet Bombs **801882F20009**
Infinite Ricochet Bombs P2 ....**80188B060009**
Infinite Specials **801882E60009**
Infinite Specials P2 ....**80188AFA0009**
Infinite Turbos **8018830A00C8**
Infinite Turbos P2 ....**80188B1E00C8**
Rapid Fire **801882FE0000**
Rapid Fire P2 ....**80188B120000**

VIEWPOINT

Always Have Sideguns **801C243C0001**
Always Have Sideguns **801C243E0001**
Always Have Sideguns **801C25600001**
Always Have Sideguns **801C25620001**
Always Have Sideguns **801C24A20180**
Always Have Sideguns **801C24A40180**
Always Have Sideguns **801C24A60180**
Always Have Sideguns **801C24A80180**
Infinite Credits **801FFFA80006**
Infinite Lives **801C29220006**
Infinite Shield In Easy Mode **801C1FAE0003**
Master Code **D00564E001E0**

VIRTUAL POOL

Always P1 Turn **800DAA640000**
Always P2 Turn **800DAA640001**
P1 Always Scratches **D00DAA640000**
P1 Always Scratches **800A65D40001**
P2 Always Scratches **D00DAA640001**
P2 Always Scratches **800A65D40001**
P1 Scratch Ball Not Spotted **D00DAA640000**
P1 Scratch Ball Not Spotted **800A65D40000**
P2 Scratch Ball Not Spotted **D00DAA640001**
P2 Scratch Ball Not Spotted **800A65D40000**

VMX RACING

Points Becker **8016426000FF**
Points Cooper **8016235000FF**
Points Duncan **801632D800FF**
Points Emitt **801613C800FF**

VR BASEBALL '97
Away Team Scores 0 ....8005BEF00000
Field of Dreams Field 8005B09A0001
Home Team Scores 0 ....8005BEEC0000

VR FOOTBALL '98
Home Team Scores 0 .... 800C602E0000
Home Team Scores 99 .... 800C602E0063

VR SOCCER
Away Team Scores 0..................... 8011B9780000
Home Team Scores 0 ....8011B9740000

US.
Infinite Heatlh PI 801435A4012C
Low Health PI 801435A40000
Infinite Health P2 ....80144A1C012C
Low Health P2 ....80144A1C0000

WAR GODS
Extra Damage PI 800992800001
Extra Damage P2 800992840001
Infinite Credits 800985800005
Infinite Health PI 800992780001
Infinite Health P2 ....8009927C0001
Infinite Time 8009E1140064

WARCRAFT II
Infinite Gold Humans 800101C8270F
Infinite Gold Orcs.................... 800101C4270F
Infinite Lumber Humans 80010188270F
Infinite Lumber Orcs 80010184270F
Infinite Oil Humans.................. 80010208270F
Infinite Oil Orcs 80010204270F

WARHAMMER
Infinite Cash 800DB920270F

WARHAWK
Infinite Lock-On Missiles 801B8A440008
Infinite Plasma Cannons 801B8A482003
Infinite Rockets 801B8A420064
Infinite Shields 801A2B3C012C

Infinite Shields 801A2B3E012C
Infinite Shields 801A2B40012C
Infinite Shields 801A2B42012C
Infinite Swarm Missiles 801B8A460012

WILD ARMS

Infinite Bullets Rudy 801341500008
Infinite Gella 801341DCFFFF
Infinite HP Cecilia .80133E580500
Infinite HP Jack 80133E240500
Infinite HP Rudy 80133DF00500
Infinite MP Cecilia .80133E5C03E7
Infinite MP Jack 80133E2803E7
Quick Level Gain Cecilia 80133E74FFFF
Quick Level Gain Jack 80133E40FFFF
Quick Level Gain Rudy 80133E0CFFFF

WIPEOUT

Enable Rapier Levels D01F701A0101
Enable Rapier Levels 801F70460101
Enable Rapier Mode D01F701A0001
Enable Rapier Mode 801F701A0101
Infinite Race Restarts D01F70140802
Infinite Race Restarts 801F70140803
Infinite Turbo Level I C013C5BAFF00
Infinite Turbo Level I 8013C5BAFF09

WIPEOUT XL

Infinite Energy 300945290001
Piranha Team 801FE4AC0100
Track Select 801FE4D20001

WWF IN YOUR HOUSE

Infinite Health PI 8006F4A00078
Infinite Health P2 . . . . .8006F4A80078
No Health P2 . . . . .8006F4A80000

XEVIOUS 3D

Infinite Lives (Xevious 3D) 8012DD580006
Weapon Power Up (X 3D) 80131EA40002

Saturn

ALBERT ODYSSEY

Master Code	F6000914C305
Master Code	B60028000000
Infinite Gold	16036936FFFF
Quick Level Gain Pike	160366B2FFFF
Quick Level Gain Eka	160366E6FFFF
Quick Level Gain Leos	1603671AFFFF
Quick Level Gain Gryzz	1603674EFFFF

ALIEN TRILOGY

Master Code	F6000914C305
Master Code	B60028000000
Acid Vest	1606CE2A0064
Auto-Mapper	1606CE260084
Flamer	1605AB0A001E
Flamer Fuel	1606CE3A001E
Infinite Batteries	1606CE420001
Infinite Bullets	1606CE2E000F
Infinite Charges	1606CE400002
Infinite Grenades	1606CE380005
Infinite Health	1606CE280064
Pulse Rifle	1605AB020001
Pulse Rifle Ammo	1606CE340040
Shotgun	1605AAFE003C
Shotgun Shells	1606CE320028
Smart Gun	1605AB060064
Smart Gun Ammo	1606CE3C0064

ALL STAR BASEBALL '97

Master Code	F6000914C305
Master Code	B60028000000
Home Team Scores 25	160AE1721900
Away Team Scores 25	160AE1720019

ANDRETTI RACING

Master Code	F6000914C305
Master Code	B60028000000
Qualify in First	160B37860064
Infinite Fuel P1	160B37A62CDA
Infinite Fuel P2	160B3C063D40

Indestructable Tires PI **160B38F6FFFF**
Indestructable Tires PI **160B3906FFFF**
Indestructable Tires PI **160B3916FFFF**
Indestructable Tires PI **160B3926FFFF**
Indestructable Tires P2 ....**160B3056FFFF**
Indestructable Tires P2 ....**160B3D66FFFF**
Indestructable Tires P2 ....**160B3D76FFFF**
Indestructable Tires P2 ....**160B3D86FFFF**

ARCADES GREATEST HITS
Master Code **F6000914C305**
Master Code **B60028000000**
Infinite Lives PI (Defender I) **360EA4110003**
Infinite Smart Bombs PI (Defender I) **360CA4130003**
Infinite Lives P2 (Defender I) **360EA44E0003**
Infinite Smart Bombs P2 (Defender I) **360CA4500003**
Infinite Lives PI (Joust) **360BA2990004**
Infinite Lives PI (Joust) **360BA29A0005**
Infinite Lives P2 (Joust) **360BA2A30004**
Infinite Lives P2 (Joust) **360BA2A40005**
Infinite Lives PI (Robotron) **360BC0340004**
Infinite Lives P2 (Robotron) **360BC0700003**

ASTAL
Master Code **F60B6C12C305**
Unlimited Energy **360DBD380005**

BASES LOADED
Master Code **F6000914C305**
Master Code **B60028000000**
Opponent Scores 0 ....**1600DEBC0000**

BATMAN FOREVER
Master Code **F6000914C305**
Master Code **B60028000000**
Infinite Health PI **160B806A0014**

BATTLE ARENA TOSHINDEN REMIX
Master Code **F6000914C305**
Master Code **B60028000000**
Infinite Health PI **160655780380**
Infinite Health P2 ....**160669B00380**

BATTLE ARENA TOSHINDEN URA

Master Code	F6000914C305
Master Code	B60028000000
Extra Characters	16057EE60010
Infinite Health P1	160723A20200
Infinite Health P2	1607476E0200

BATTLE MONSTERS

Master Code	F6000914C305
Master Code	B60028000000
Infinite Health P1	160377F00064
Infinite Health P2	160378F80064

BATTLE STATIONS

Master Code	F6000914C305
Master Code	B60028000000
Infinite Energy P1	16067C920064
Infinite Energy P2	16067FC20064

BIG HURT BASEBALL

Master Code	F6000914C305
Master Code B	B60028000000
Player 1 Always Wins	160ADBA80500

BLACK DAWN

Master Code	F6000914C305
Master Code	B60028000000
Infinite Missiles	102B96300064
Infinite Napalm	102B96340064
Infinite Rockets	102B96320064
Infinite TAC	102B96360064

BOTTOM OF THE 9TH

Master Code	F6000914C305
Master Code	B60028000000
Away Team Wins	1605BD782500
Away Team Wins	1605BD8C2500
Home Team Wins	1605BD780025
Home Team Wins	1605BD8C0025

BUBBLE BOBBLE
Master Code F6000914C305
Master Code B60028000000
Infinite Lives (Bubble Bobble) 1604FDE00002
Infinite Lives (Rainbow Islands) 160442AA0003

CASPER
Master Code F6000942C305
Master Code B60028000000
Infinite Brass Keys 1604D012FFFF
Infinite Fools Gold 1604D016FFFF
Infinite Health 160D808EFFFF
Infinite Iron Keys 1604D00EFFFF

CLOCKWORK KNIGHT
Master Code F6000914C305
Master Code B60028000000
Infinite Health (Must Use w/ Inf. Time) 36043CB40005
Infinite Lives 16043CBC0004
Infinite Time 360587A200FE

COLLEGE SLAM
Master Code F6000914C305
Master Code B60028000000
Opponent Scores 0 ....16066EFE0000

COMMAND & CONQUER
Master Code F6000914C305
Master Code B60028000000
Infinite Money 160E656207D0
Infinite Money 160E6C4A07D0

CONTRA
Master Code F6000914C305
Master Code B60028000000
Infinite Health P1 ....1609DEDC0008
Infinite Health P2 ....1609DF080008
Infinite Bombs P1 ....1609DEDE0008
Infinite Bombs P2 ....1609DF0A0008

73

CORPSE KILLER

Master Code	F6000914C305
Master Code	B60028000000
Infinite Bullets	16050D0C0063
Infinite Health	16050D080063

CRITICOM

Master Code	F6000914C305
Master Code	B60028000000
Infinite Health P1	102FFA240320
Infinite Health P2	102FF6FC0320
No Health P2	102FF6FC0000

CROC

Master Code	F6000914C305
Master Code	B60028000000
Infinite Crystals	16052E3E0063
Infinite Lives	1605D112000A
6 Gobbos Saved	16052E460006

CROW

Master Code	F6000914C305
Master Code	B60028000000
Infinite Health	1606A82A007F

CRUSADER

Master Code	F6000914C305
Master Code	B60028000000
EMP Inhibitor	160DBDAC0100
Grenade Launcher	160DBE040100
Infinite Cash	160DBE34FFFF
Infinite Det Pacs	160DBDBC0900
Infinite Energy	160DBE2E09C4
Infinite Grenades	160DBE20040B
Infinite Health	160DBE2C0078
Infinite Limpet Mines	160DBDC40900
Infinite RP Ammo	160DBE24093C
Infinite Shotgun Ammo	160DBE28040B
Infinite Spider Bombs	160DBDC80900
Laser Rifle	160DBDF40100
RP-32	160DBDE80100
Shotgun	160DBDEC0100

CRYPT KILLER

Master Code	F6000914C305
Master Code	B60028000000
Infinite Health P1	160A6E240003
Infinite Credits	160A6E140200

CYBER SPEEDWAY

Master Code	F6000914C305
Master Code	B60028000000
Infinite Rockets	1609E5980005
Infinite Rockets	160D3AD20005

D

Master Code	F6000914C305
Master Code	B60028000000
Infinite Mirror Hints	1601F8420001
Infinite Time	1601F80A1A60

DARIUS GAIDEN

Master Code	F6000914C305
Master Code	B60028000000
Full Weapons P2	160D3520000E
Infinite Bombs P1	160D34A60005
Infinite Bombs P2	160D351E0005
Infinite Credits P1	160D34CE0003
Infinite Credits P2	160D35460003

DARK LEGEND

Master Code	F6000914C305
Master Code	B60028000000
Infinite Energy P1	1609FE2C0080

DARK SAVIOR

Master Code	F6000924FFFF
Infinite Points	102FB02EFFFF
Infinite HP Garian	160DEFB003E7
Infinite HP Garian	160DEFB203E7
Infinite B-HP Garian	160DEFB603E7

DARKLIGHT CONFLICT
Master Code F6000915C305
Master Code B60028000000
Infinite Energy 16071A901E00

DAYTONA CCE
Master Code F6000924FFFF
Place 1st 160511F80100
Race as Uma 102FC21C0009
Race as Uma2 ....102FC21C000A

DAYTONA USA
Master Code F6000914C305
Master Code B60028000000
Infinite Time (Arcade Mode) 1607EAAE0318
Number of Cars on Course 1=5 160480720005
Number of Cars on Course 2=5 160480740005
Number of Cars on Course 3=5 160480760005
Number of Laps on Course 3=6 ....1604805E0006
Number of Laps on Course 1=16 ....1604805A0010
Number of Laps on Course 2=10 ....1604805C000A

DIE HARD ARCADE
Master Code F6000914C305
Master Code B60028000000
Infinite Credits 1609FD74FF00

DOOM
Master Code F6000914C305
Master Code B60028000000
Infinite Bullets 160893CA03E7
Infinite Shotgun Shells 160893CE03E7
Infinite Rockets 160893D605FF
Infinite Plasma 160893D205FF
Chainsaw 160893C60001
Shotgun 160893AE0001
Double Barrel Shotgun 160893B20001

Chaingun	160893B60001
Rocket Launcher	160893BA0001
Plasma Rifle	160893BE0001
BFG 9000	160893C00001
Red Key	1608937A0001
Yellow Key	160893800001
Blue Key	1608937C0001
Rapid Fire	160894260001

FIGHTERS MEGAMIX

Master Code	F6000914C305
Master Code	B60028000000
Infinite Health PI	1606552C00FA
Infinite Health P2	1606732C00FA
No Health PI	1606552C0000
No Health P2	1606732C0000

FIGHTING VIPERS

Master Code	F6000914C305
Master Code	B60028000000
Infinite Health PI	1606282800FA
Infinite Health PI	160945A000FA
Infinite Health P2	1606472800FA
Infinite Health P2	160945A400FA
Infinite Time	160E005E0781
No Health P2	160647280000
No Health P2	160945A40000

GALACTIC ATTACK

Master Code	F6000914C305
Master Code	B60028000000
Infinite Armor PI	160EAC907F9F
Infinite Armor P2	160EAD907F9F
Infinite Credits	160DC70C0004
Infinite Lives PI	160EAC300003
Infinite Lives P2	160EAD300003
Level 9 Weapon PI	160EAC320800
Level 9 Weapon P2	160EAD320800

GALAXY FIGHT

Master Code	F6000914C305
Master Code	B60028000000
Infinite Health PI	16063258FFFF
Infinite Health P2	1606344CFFFF

GEX

Master Code	F6000914C305
Master Code	B60028000000
Infinite Lives	160703160099

GHEN WAR

Master Code	F606B124C305
Master Code	B60028000000
Infinite Lives	160948F03C64
Infinite Lock-On Rockets	3609491E0064
Infinite Mines	360949200006
Infinite Robots	360949210006
Infinite Rockets	3609491F0008

GOLDEN AXE

Master Code	F6000914C305
Master Code	B60028000000
Infinite Health PI	16078A5C0080
Infinite Health P2	16078B500080

GUARDIAN HEROES

Master Code	F6000924C305
Master Code	B60028000000
Begin at High Level	16033C7400C0
Infinite Lives PI	1601DBA40900

HANG-ON GP

Master Code	F6000914C305
Master Code	B60028000000
Infinite Time	1604BCE2003C

HYPER 3D PINBALL
Master Code F6000914C305
Master Code B60028000000
Infinite Balls 1604F37A0001

IMPACT RACING
Master Code F6000924C305
Double Laser 160DC1B66402
Fire Wall 160DC18E0101
Heat Seeking Missile Launcher 160DC18C0101
Infinite Fire Fuel .160DC1A20063
Infinite Heat Seekers 160DC19A0063
Infinite Mines 160DC19E0063
Infinite Missiles .160DC1960063
Infinite Smart Bombs 160DC1A60063
Lasers Never Overheat 102457120000
Missile Launcher 160DC18C0100
Quad Laser 160DC1B66404
Smart Bomb Launcher 160DC1900101

IN THE HUNT
Master Code F6000914C305
Master Code B60028000000
Infinite Armor P1 . . . . .1607D5EA0001
Infinite Armor P2 . . . . .1607D4EA0001
Infinite Credits .1607C9A80009
Infinite Time 160922AC0064

IRON STORM
Master Code F6000914C305
Master Code B60028000000
Infinite Cash 1603BCB2FFFF
Build Units Anywhere D60060340001
Build Units Anywhere 160DE6E00001

JOHNNY BAZOOKATONE
Master Code F6000914C305
Master Code B60028000000
Infinite Lives 10288EE60008

LAST BRONX

Master Code	F6000914C305
Master Code	B60028000000
Infinite Health P1	160955B80090
Infinite Health P2	160955DC0090
Play as Red Eye	1606F0880008

LEGEND OF OASIS

Master Code	F6000914C305
Master Code	B60028000000
Infinite Health	16088DA20FF0
Infinite Magic	16088DA60FFF
Scroll of Miracle Rod	160887120900
Scroll of Sound	160887160900

LOST WORLD

Master Code	F6000914C305
Master Code	B60028000000
Full Instinct	1600414800FF
Infinite Health	1606508A007F

MACHINE HEAD

Master Code	F6000914C305
Master Code	B60028000000
Infinite Armor	160B9CB200FB
Infinite Armor	160BE37E00FB
Infinite Disruptor	160BE50A000A
Infinite Flamethrower	160BE4F600FA
Infinite Grenades	160BE506000A
Infinite Homing Missiles	160BE4FE000A
Infinite Io-Storm	160BE50E000A
Infinite Missiles	160BE4FA0014
Infinite Photon	160BE502000A

MADDEN '97

Master Code	F6000924C305
Master Code	B60028000000
Extra Teams	1605510A006B
Infinite Time Outs Home	1605B97E0004
Infinite Time Outs Away	160599BE0004
Home Team Scores 0	1605B97C0000
Away Team Scores 0	160599BC0000

MANX TT SUPERBIKE
Master Code	F6000914C305
Master Code	B60028000000
Place 1st	1606F3DA0000
Infinite Time	16088A7E02CE

MARVEL SUPER HEROES
Master Code	F6000924FFFF
Infinite Health P1	160949FC0090
Infinite Health P2	160A644C0090

MASS DESTRUCTION
Master Code	F6000914C305
Master Code	B60028000000
Hi-Explosive Cannon	1606059A0100
Infinite Hi-Explosive Shells	16060598270F
Mine Bay	160605A60100
Infinite Mines	160605A4270F
Mortar	160605A00100
Infinite Mortar Shells	1606059E270F
Torus Bombs	160605AC0100
Infinite Torus Bombs	160605AA270F
Flame Thrower	160605B20100
Infinite Flamer Fuel	160605B0270F
Guided Missile	160605B80100
Infinite Guided Missiles	160605B6270F
Infinite Armor	160663EA1770
Infinite Time	1605ACD80007

MAXIMUM FORCE
Master Code	F6000914C305
Master Code	B60028000000
No Reload P1	160862760008
Infinite Credits P1	160864AE0009
Infinite Health P1	160862220005
Machine Gun P1	160862720001
Shotgun P1	160862720002
No Reload P2	160863020008
Infinite Credits P2	160864B20009
Infinite Health P2	160862AE0005
Machine Gun P2	160862FE0001
Shotgun P2	160862FE0002

MECHWARRIOR 2

Master Code	.F6000914C305
Master Code	.B60028000000
Never Overheat	.16030AC00000
Infinite Ammo	.160301BA005A
Infinite Ammo	.160301D2005A
Infinite Ammo	.160301EA005A
Infinite Ammo	.16030202005A
Infinite Ammo	.1603021A005A
Infinite Ammo	.16030232005A
Infinite Ammo	.1603024A005A
Infinite Ammo	.16030262005A
Infinite Ammo	.1603027A005A
Super Code	.102E243AFFFF

MEGA MAN 8

Master Code	.F6000914C305
Master Code	.B60028000000
Have Mega Ball	.160361E40100
Infinite Mega Balls	.160361E62800
Have Flash Bomb	.160361E80100
Infinite Flash Bombs	.160361EA2800
Have Thunder Claw	.160361EC0100
Infinite Thunder Claws	.160361EE2800
Have Ice Wave	.160361F00100
Infinite Ice Waves	.160361F22800
Have Tornado Hold	.160361F40100
Infinite Tornado Hold	.160361F62800
Have Water Balloon	.160361F80100
Infinite Water Balloons	.160361FA2800
Have Flame Sword	.160361FC0100
Infinite Flame Sword	.160361FE2800
Have Homing Sniper	.160362000100
Infinite Homing Snipers	.160362022800
Have Astro Crush	.160362040100
Infinite Astro Crush	.160362062800

MINNESOTA FATS POOL

Master Code	.F6000914C305
Master Code	.B60028000000
Always Player 1's Turn	.160AA53E0000

MORTAL KOMBAT II

Master Code	.F6000914C305
Master Code	.B60028000000
Infinite Health P1	.160BDB7000A1

MORTAL KOMBAT III

Master Code	F6017718C305
Master Code	B60028000000
Infinite Health P1	160D19FC00A6
Infinite Health P2	160D20D800A6
No Health P2	160D20D80000

MORTAL KOMBAT TRILOGY

Master Code	F6000914C305
Master Code	B60028000000
Infinite Health P1	16083ED400A6
No Health P1	16083ED40000
Infinite Health P2	1608404C00A6
No Health P2	1608404C0000

NASCAR '98

Master Code	F6000914C305
Master Code	B60028000000
Low Lap Time	102B8556006B

NBA ACTION

Master Code	F6000914C305
Master Code	B60028000000
Away Team Scores 0	160849FA0000
Home Team Scores 0	160F38400000

NBA JAM EXTREME

Master Code	F6000914C305
Master Code	B60028000000
Away Team Scores 0	1602E44A0000
Home Team Scores 0	1602E4460000
Infinite Turbo P1	160A0B6A00FF
Infinite Turbo P2	160A0C5600FF
Infinite Turbo P3	160A0D4200FF
Infinite Turbo P4	160A0E2E00FF

NBA JAM TE

Master Code	F6000914C305
Master Code	B60028000000
Player 1 Scores 9	1606C0020009
Player 2 Scores 0	1606C00A0000

NBA LIVE '97

Master Code	F6000914C305
Master Code	B60028000000
Home Team Scores 0	1609D0760000
Away Team Scores 0	1609D1760000
Maximum Fatigue	160835C600FF
Maximum Field Goals	160835E600FF
Maximum 3-Pointers	1608360600FF
Maximum Free Throws	1608362600FF
Maximum Dunking	1608364600FF
Maximum Stealing	1608366600FF
Maximum Blocking	1608368600FF
Maximum Offensive Rebounds	160836A600FF
Maximum Defensive Rebounds	160836C600FF
Maximum Passing	160836E600FF
Maximum Offensive Awareness	1608370600FF
Maximum Defensive Awareness	1608372600FF
Maximum Speed	1608374600FF
Maximum Quickness	1608376600FF
Maximum Jumping	1608378600FF
Maximum Dribbling	160837A600FF
Maximum Strength	160837C600FF
Maximum Shot Range	160837E600FF

NBA LIVE '98

Master Code	F6000914C305
Master Code	B60028000000
Home Team Scores 0	160AF7220000
Away Team Scores 0	160AF9C60000
Home Team Scores 150	160AF7220096

NFL '97

Master Code	F6000914C305
Master Code	B60028000000
Home Team Scores 0	16095A8A0000
Home Team Scores 0	16095A960000

NFL QUARTERBACK CLUB

Master Code	F6000924C305
Master Code	B60028000000
Player 2 Scores 0	1603EC540000

NHL ALL-STAR HOCKEY

Master Code	F6000914C305
Master Code	B60028000000
Enable Code (Must Be On)	D6043888414E
Player I Scores 99	3608BD340063
Player 2 Scores 0	3608BD350000

NORSE BY NORSEWEST

Master Code	F6000914C305
Master Code	B60028000000
Infinite Health Erik	16073B7E0003
Infinite Health Baleog	16073B9A0003
Infinite Health Olaf	16073BB60003

PANDEMONIUM

Master Code	F6000914C305
Master Code	B60028000000
Infinite Credits	160660680302
Infinite Health	1606606A0200

PANZER DRAGOON

Master Code	F6000914C305
Master Code	B60028000000
Infinite Credits	16084BAA0005
Infinite Energy	1607FB080100

PANZER DRAGOON II

Master Code	F6000914C305
Master Code	B60028000000
3 Way Shot	1607335C0100
5 Way Shot	1607335C0200
Graviton Shot	1607335C0600
Homing Shot	1607335C0500

POWERSLAVE

Master Code	F6000914C305
Master Code	B60028000000
All-Seeing Eye	1605186E0001
All Keys	1604A556FFFF
All Weapons and Artifacts	1608607EFFFF
Infinite Flame Thrower Ammo	160860A200E0
Infinite Health	1608608A00C8
Infinite M-60 Ammo	1608609A001E
Infinite Manacle Ammo	160860AE0004
Infinite Pistol Ammo	16086096003C
Infinite Ring of Ra Ammo	160860AA00E0
Transmitter	1608607CFFFF

PRIMAL RAGE

Master Code	F6000914C305
Master Code	B60028000000
Infinite Health P1	160F9A3A0000
Infinite Health P1	160F9F980000
Infinite Health P2	160F9A4C0000
Infinite Health P2	160F9ACE0000

RESIDENT EVIL

Master Code	F6000914C305
Master Code	B60028000000
Crate o' Goodies	D02F867C00A0
Crate o' Goodies	102F87240BFF
Crate o' Goodies	102F87260CFF
Crate o' Goodies	102F87280DFF
Crate o' Goodies	102F872A0EFF
Crate o' Goodies	102F872C0FFF
Crate o' Goodies	102F872E10FF
Crate o' Goodies	102F873011FF
Crate o' Goodies	102F873212FF
Crate o' Goodies	102F873446FF
Crate o' Goodies	102F873647FF
Crate o' Goodies	102F873848FF
Infinite Health	102F51AC008C
Weapons in Crate at Start	D02F867C00A0
Weapons in Crate at Start	102F877A030F
Weapons in Crate at Start	102F877C040F
Weapons in Crate at Start	102F877E060F
Weapons in Crate at Start	102F8780070F
Weapons in Crate at Start	102F87820A0F
Weapons in Crate at Start	102F8778050F
Weapons in Crate at Start	102F8776080F
Weapons in Crate at Start	102F8774090F

Health Restored with X Button **D02FF8460008**
Health Restored with X Button **102F51AC008C**
Health Restored with X Button **102F867E008C**

REVOLUTION X
Master Code . . . . **.F6000914C305**
Master Code . . . . **.B60028000000**
Infinite Credits . . . . **.160E9CFA0063**

ROAD RASH
Master Code . . . . **.F6000914C305**
Master Code . . . . **.B60028000000**
Have Stiletto Bike . . . . **.160740740709**
Infinite Cash . . . . **.1607407EFFFF**

ROBO PIT
Master Code . . . . **.F6000914C305**
Master Code . . . . **.B60028000000**
Infinite Health P1 . . . . **.1609D6980090**
Infinite Health P1 . . . . **.1609D6E80090**
Infinite Health P2 . . . . **.160A09E40090**
Infinite Health P2 . . . . **.160AA7EA0090**
No Health P2 . . . . **.160A09E40000**
No Health P2 . . . . **.160AA7EA0000**

ROBOTICA
Master Code **F601821CC305**
Infinite Fuel . . . . **.160CFBEA03E7**
Infinite Laser . . . . **.160CFBFA0014**
Infinite Missiles . . . . **.160CFC000005**
Infinite Vulcan Ammo . . . . **.160CFBF403E7**

SCUD
Master Code . . . . **.F6000914C305**
Master Code . . . . **.B60028000000**
Infinite Health P1 . . . . **.1603AADC0000**
Infinite Health P2 . . . . **.1603AAF20000**
Infinite Credits . . . . **.160ED9AC0009**
Spread Shot P1 . . . . **.160452EA0003**
Spread Shot P2 . . . . **.160454720003**

SEGA TOURING CAR
Master Code........................	F6000924FFFF
Low Course Time....................	160066640000
Low Course Time....................	1600666C0000
Infinite Time	1600669A0244

SHELLSHOCK
Master Code	F6000914C305
Master Code	B60028000000
Air Support	160707480001
Chain Gun Coolant	160707520004
Engine Upgrade	1607074A0004
Extra Armor	1607073E0006
Infinite Cash	16070756FFFF
Reload Mechanism	1607074E0004
SAM Missiles	160707420004
Targeting Computer	160707500004
Track Upgrade	1607074C0004

SHINING WISDOM
Master Code	F6000914C305
Master Code	B60028000000
Have Healing Herb	3600611A0001
Have Mole Claw	360061430001
Have Monkey Suit	360061420001
Have Pegasus Helm	360061460001
Have Shining Sword	3600613C0001
Have Slide Shoes	3600613E0001
Infinite Health	1600615A003B
Infinite Money	160061142500

SHINOBI
Master Code	F602ADD4C305
Master Code	B60028000000
Infinite Daggers	160252B60063
Infinite Health	160EA2FCFFFF
Infinite Lives	160252B80009
Infinite Thunder Dragons	160252BE0001
Mega Jumps	160EA2CE0000

SIM CITY 2000
Master Code	P6000914C305
Master Code	B60028000000
Unlimited Money	1607AEE83B9B
Unlimited Money	1607AEEA0F00

SKELETON WARRIORS

Master Code	.P6000914C305
Master Code	.B60028000000
Infinite Health	.1607EBB60064
Infinite Lives	.1607EBBE0064
Infinite Starsword	.1607EBCA0064

SLAM-N-JAM

Master Code	.F6000914C305
Master Code	.B60028000000
Away Team Scores 0	.1025B8780000
Home Team Scores 0	.1025B6740000

SONIC JAM

Master Code	F6000914C305
Master Code	B60028000000
99 Rings	160FFE200063

SONIC R

Master Code	F6000914C305
Master Code	B60028000000
99 Rings	1600B3F00063
Place 1st in Grand Prix Race	1600B4340001

SONIC 3D BLAST

Master Code	.F6000914C305
Master Code	.B60028000000
Infinite Lives	.16097C2E0009

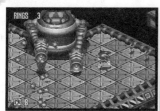

SOVIET STRIKE

Master Code F6000914C305
Master Code B60028000000
Infinite Armor 16070D2A270F
Infinite Fuel 16070E3A6400

SPOT GOES TO HOLLYWOOD

Master Code F6000914C305
Master Code B60028000000
Have 5 Stars 16066FB4001F
Infinite Lives 160694C20009

STAR FIGHTER

Master Code F6000914C305
Master Code B60028000000
Infinite Armor 1608330A0040
Infinite ATA Missiles 160BF4F203E7
Infinite ATG Missiles 160BF4EE03E7
Infinite Beam Lasers 160BF4FA03E7
Infinite Mega-Bombs 160BF4F603E7
Infinite Mines 160BF50203E7
Infinite Multi-Missiles 160BF4FE03E7

STEEP SLOPE SLIDERS

Master Code........................F6000914C305
Master Code........................B60028000000
Infinite Time 1607FEE601F0
Extra Points 160808560FFF

TETRIS PLUS

Master Code........................F6000914C305
Master Code........................B60028000000
No Timer 160D20B20001
Pause 160D18120010
Pause 160D20020055

THEME PARK

Master Code	F6000914C305
Master Code	B60028000000
Infinite Cash	160DF7840FFF
Infinite Cash	160DF7860FFF

THREE DIRTY DWARVES

Master Code	F6000914C305
Master Code	B60028000000
Infinite Skulls	1604B85E0007

TOMB RAIDER

Master Code	F6000736C305
Master Code	B60028000000
Infinite Health	10245F7A03E8
Infinite Health	1023A5FE03E8
Infinite Health	1022DFA203E8
Infinite Health	1025DE4203E8
Infinite Health	1023C91A03E8
Infinite Health	1024426A03E8
Infinite Health	1022210E03E8
Infinite Health	1021BBC203E8
Infinite Health	1021546203E8
Infinite Health	1022D2A603E8
Infinite Health	102262F203E8
Infinite Health	102356DA03E8
Infinite Health	1022594203E8
Infinite Health	1022D54A03E8
Infinite Health	1022AB1E03E8
Infinite Air	1609447E0708
Infinite Shotgun Shells	1609452A0030
Infinite Medic Packs	16022D000040
Infinite Magnum Ammo	16094512001B
Infinite Uzi Ammo	1609451E0128
Final Level	16060CB6000F

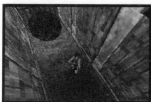

TUNNEL B1
Master Code	F6000914C305
Infinite Energy	16058B680320
Infinite Lives	16058B600320
Infinite Boosters	16058B6C0003

VIRTUA COP
Master Code	F6003DEEC305
Master Code	B60028000000
Infinite Bullets P1	1606A3E80006
Infinite Bullets P2	1606A3980006
Infinite Health P1	160579520505
Infinite Health P2	160579120505
Machine Gun P1	1606A3AE5DAC
Machine Gun P2	1606A3FE5DAC

VIRTUA FIGHTER
Master Code	F6000914C304
Master Code	B60028000000
Enable Code (Must Be On)	0601EDCE0009
Infinite Energy P1	16092072FFFF
Infinite Energy P2	160940CEFFFF

VIRTUA FIGHTER II
Master Code	F6000914C305
Master Code	B60028000000
Allow Out Of Ring Fighting	160E0068004F
Infinite Energy P1	160621B800A0
Infinite Time	160E00320782
Low Gravity	160E007A0024
Mega Kick	160E007C0000
Play Bonus Level 10	160E00020A0A
Play Under Water	160E001A0002
Play Under Water	160E00380010

VIRTUA FIGHTER KIDS

Master Code	F6000914C305
Master Code	B60028000000
Infinite Health P1	1604597400A0
Infinite Health P2	16046A7400A0

VIRTUA FIGHTER REMIX

Master Code	F6000914C305
Master Code	B60028000000
Infinite Energy P1	1609207200A0
Play Bonus Level	1609EA900909

VIRTUA RACING

Master Code	F6000914C305
Master Code	B60028000000
Only One Lap	16074ED40003

VR SOCCER

Master Code	F6000914C305
Master Code	B60028000000
Team B Scores 0	1608DDDE0000

WARCRAFT II

Master Code	F6000914C305
Master Code	B60028000000
Infinite Gold (Humans)	160D564A270F
Infinite Gold (Orcs)	160D5646270F
Infinite Lumber (Humans)	160D560A270F
Infinite Lumber (Orcs)	160D5606270F
Infinite Oil (Humans)	160D568A270F
Infinite Oil (Orcs)	160D5686270F

WING ARMS
Master Code. F6000914C305

Master Code B60028000000
Infinite Credits 160654DC0009
Infinite Missiles 160659320064
Rapid Missile Fire .160659260004

WIPEOUT
Master Code F6000914C305
Master Code B60028000000
Rapier Class 160622A20101

WORLD SERIES BASEBALL
Master Code F6000914C305
Master Code B60028000000
Player 1 Scores 20 . . . . .160F41960014
Player 2 Scores 0 .160F41760000
Unlimited Balls 1607ACF60000
Unlimited Strikes .1607ACF40000

WORLD SERIES BASEBALL 2
Master Code F6000914C305
Master Code B60028000000
Away Team Wins .160F41BA0032
Home Team Wins .160F419A0032

WORLD SERIES BASEBALL '98
Master Code F6000914C305
Master Code B60028000000
Away Team Wins .102F003E0032
Home Team Wins .102F001E0032
Infinite Strikes .160837820000
Don't Touch That Ball 160840EE0001

WWF IN YOUR HOUSE
Master Code F6000914C305
Master Code B60028000000
infinite Health P1 . . . . .16030DE00055
Infinite Health P1 . . . . .16030DE20055
Infinite Health P2 . . . . .16030E000055
Infinite Health P2 . . . . .16030E020055
No Health P2 . . . . .16030E000000
No Health P2 . . . . .16030E020000